DATE DUE

Oklahoma's Governors, 1929-1955: Depression to Prosperity

Volume XIX
The Oklahoma Series

Oklahoma's Governors, 1929-1955:

Depression
to
Prosperity

EDITED BY
LeRoy H. Fischer
Oppenheim Professor of History
Oklahoma State University
Stillwater, Oklahoma

Bob L. Blackburn, Series Editor
Oklahoma Historical Society
Oklahoma City, Oklahoma
1983

Library of Congress Catalog Card No: 83-060261

Fischer, LeRoy H.
   Oklahoma's Governors, 1929-1955: Depression to Prosperity

   1. *Oklahoma—History.* 2. *Oklahoma—Political History.* 3. *Oklahoma—Biographies.* I. *Title.* II.
Series.

ISBN 0-941498-34-4
ISBN 0-941498-35-2 *(pbk.)*

CONTENTS

CONTRIBUTORS

SARA L. BERNSON is a brokerage assistant with Provident Life and Accident Insurance Company, Seattle, Washington. She completed her undergraduate study at the University of Maryland, College Park, Maryland, was awarded the Master of Arts degree by the University of South Dakota, Vermillion, South Dakota, and did additional work on the Doctor of Philosophy degree in history at Oklahoma State University.

EDDA L. BILGER is a candidate for the Doctor of Philosophy degree in history at Oklahoma State University. She did her undergraduate study at the Padagogische Hochschule, Freiburg im Breisgau, West Germany, and at Pasadena City College, Pasadena, California. Her Master of Arts degree in history was awarded by Oklahoma State University.

WILLIAM P. CORBETT teaches history at Northern Oklahoma College, Tonkawa, Oklahoma. He completed his undergraduate degree at Clarion State College, Clarion, Pennsylvania, and the Master of Arts degree in history at the University of South Dakota, Vermillion, South Dakota. His Doctor of Philosophy degree in history was awarded by Oklahoma State University.

MICHAEL W. EVERMAN is a Doctor of Philosophy degree candidate in history at Oklahoma State University and works as information specialist with the Missouri Cultural Heritage Center, University of Missouri, Columbia, Missouri. He completed the undergraduate degree at Cameron University, Lawton, Oklahoma, and the Master of Arts degree in history at Oklahoma State University.

LeROY H. FISCHER, the editor of this book, is Oppenheim Professor of History at Oklahoma State University. In addition to numerous articles, he is the author or editor of eight books.

MAYNARD J. HANSON is a Doctor of Philosophy degree candidate in history at Oklahoma State University. He earned his undergraduate degree at Yankton College, Yankton, South Dakota, and the Master of Arts degree in history at the University of South Dakota, Vermillion, South Dakota.

JIM L. MYERS is a journalist with the *Tulsa World*, Tulsa, Oklahoma. He holds two undergraduate degrees from Oklahoma State University as well as the Master of Arts degree in history from the same institution.

COURTNEY ANN VAUGHN-ROBERSON teaches in the College of Education at the University of Oklahoma, Norman, Oklahoma. Her undergraduate degree was awarded by the University of Kansas, Lawrence, Kansas, the Master of Education degree by Central State University, Edmond, Oklahoma, the Master of Arts degree in history by Oklahoma State University, and the Doctor of Education degree also by Oklahoma State University.

PREFACE

Biographical studies of Oklahoma's governors before and since statehood, even of journal article length, generally remain undone. Almost without exception, book-length biographies of the governors also are not to be found. *Territorial Governors of Oklahoma*, edited by LeRoy H. Fischer and published by the Oklahoma Historical Society in 1975, was the first book publication intended, at least in part, to meet this need through article-length studies. The present book is planned to continue the same treatment, with two other volumes, for Oklahoma's state governors. The pattern is basically indentical for each of the biographies. Following the description of an unusual incident or unique condition used to introduce each of the biographical sketches, the background of the governor before election to the executive office is presented briefly. Then detailed attention is given to issues and problems of the administration. Finally, the biographee's life after service as governor is treated concisely, and in conclusion an assessment of the administration is drawn.

The studies that follow were prepared by graduate students in my research seminar at Oklahoma State University. To these people I am deeply grateful, especially for their cooperation and dedication beyond minimal requirements. Much appreciation is extended also to W. David Baird, professor and head of the History Department at Oklahoma University, for his encouragement and interest in this undertaking. Also at Oklahoma State University, Norman N. Durham, dean of the Graduate College, Smith L. Holt, dean of the College of Arts and Sciences, Richard C. Powell, director of research of the College of Arts and Sciences, and Neil J. Hackett, Jr., associate dean of the College of Arts and Sciences, likewise contributed substantially. For viewing this project with favor, special thanks are extended to C. Earle Metcalf, the executive director of the Oklahoma Historical Society; to Bob L. Blackburn, the editor and director of the Interpretations Division of the Oklahoma Historical Society; to Kenny L. Franks, former editor and publications director of the Oklahoma Historical Society; to the Interpretations Committee of the Oklahoma Historical Society; and to the Board of Directors of the Oklahoma Historical Society.

Lending additional encouragement were the late Elisabeth Oppenheim, the late Leo Oppenheim, the late George H. Shirk, Joan Oppenheim, and Edgar R. Oppenheim, all of Oklahoma City, Oklahoma. Martha, my wife, aided materially throughout the preparation of the papers for publication and for her able assistance I am most appreciative. Lastly, without the vast holdings of the Oklahoma State University Edmon Low Library and the cooperation of its capable staff, especially Heather M. Lloyd and Vicki D. Phillips, the studies could not have been completed.

LeRoy H. Fischer

Oklahoma's Governors, 1929-1955

Oklahoma's Chief Executives, 1929-1955

By LeRoy H. Fischer

William Judson Holloway (1929-1931), the first governor of the Great Depression years, like his impeached predecessor, Henry Simpson Johnston (1927-1929), was also a Democrat. He had served as the state's lieutenant governor since 1927. Unlike Johnston, he understood and mastered successful human relations and restored and maintained the credibility of Oklahoma government. He recommended to the legislature the passage of a highway bill abolishing the five highway commissioners, a source of controversy under Johnston, and the establishment of a new three-member commission. Because he had not had time to compile a legislative program, he requested that the legislators adjourn and promised to recall them. They honored both requests.

Initially, appointments took much of Holloway's time. He refused to fill vacancies for political considerations alone, for he desired to obtain only the most competent people. He selected Louis (Lew) Haynes Wentz of Ponca City for chairman of the Oklahoma Highway Commission. Wentz, a millionaire oilman and philanthropist, was a Republican, however, and possible gubernatorial candidate. Wentz did not want the chairmanship because he thought it might interfere with business affairs, but eventually consented. When Holloway completed the commission appointments with two Democrats, he believed he had placed the agency under competent supervision.

Holloway informed the special legislative session he called in May, 1929, of the need for budgetary economy and threatened to veto excessive appropriations. He also recommended and signed into law bills to bring to an end toll bridges and toll roads, to permit the highway commission to condemn and purchase such structures, to build free equivalents, and to end the franchise authority of toll corporations. Because he sensed public sentiment existed for a large highway bond issue to pave completely the 4,500 unpaved miles of state highway, he proposed an issue of $150 million. The measure as introduced in the legislature took the form of a constitutional amendment, but it also increased highway commissioner terms to six years, and this caused a partisan split in the house of representatives. The day before the scheduled vote in that body, Oklahoma Highway Commission Chairman Wentz held a banquet at the Skirvin Hotel for the Republican opponents of the proposed amendment and approved their opposition. The bill failed.

In another major area, collegiate reforms recommended by Holloway to remove substantially these institutions from politics called for a constitutional amendment creating separate boards of regents for the agricultural and mechanical colleges and for the University of Oklahoma. Although passed by the legislature, the proposed amendment was not approved by the voters. The governor also recommended that other state collegiate institutions be placed under the jurisdiction of the Oklahoma Board of Education, but the legislature did not approve the measure. Another bill, however, intended to remove duplicate programs in the colleges, passed and established a coordinating board of collegiate administrators. The governor failed to appoint its two public members and it never met.

In the related area of common schools, Holloway called for a permanent technically qualified textbook commission, a staggered system of textbook adoption, and the removal of the governor from the commission as orginally constituted in 1925. The governor also recommended centralized certification of teachers by the Oklahoma Board of Education. Both measures were approved by the legislature. Direct appropriations from state general revenue funds, begun to assist with common school financing in the 1927 legislature, continued in the 1929 legislature. The amount was increased by $250,000, but this was totally inadequate for local school districts to maintain quality education.

With regard to taxation, Holloway sought tax reform through the creation of a state tax commission to equalize assessments, investigate alternative revenue systems, and uncover tax evasion. But legislators supporting large corporations vehemently opposed a tax commission, and the governor did not pressure them. Enough money was available, however, to approve salary increases for state employees. Finally, the legislature approved a runoff primary for the state.

The Great Depression came to Oklahoma during Holloway's administration, and he used the resources of the state to alleviate its effects. Money from the federal government purchased seed for farmers through a drought relief commission, the Oklahoma School Land Office invested surplus revenues in farm land instead of bonds, weak banks received encouragement to liquidate or consolidate with stronger institutions, and the Oklahoma Highway Department, in an effort to create jobs, let as many contracts as possible.

In twenty-two months in the governor's office, Holloway had alleviated much of the political tension and confusion that existed at the time of his inauguration. He brought needed decorum and responsibility to the office of governor. Although some of his proposed reforms were rejected by the legislature or the voters, others won approval, such as improved adoption methods for textbooks, increased salaries for state employees, and centralized teacher certification. His brief service bridged the period from the prosperous twenties to the depression thirties.

The next governor, William Henry Murray (1931-1935), unlike Holloway, was controversial. He emerged as the champion of the masses of people suffering from the Great Depression, and this sincere concern brought him into the executive office. His basic program called for softening the effects of the Great Depression by decreasing taxes for lower income people, by enforcing strict governmental economy, and by aiding the destitute and unemployed.

Even before his election, Murray prepared a legislative bill establishing a tax commission, and it became law within a week following his inauguration. Thus taxes would be assessed on an equal basis and state taxes would be collected centrally. Two years later, in 1933, the voters of the state passed a constitutional amendment abolishing the state property tax, terminating the township tax, and reducing the local property tax by almost a third. To compensate for the loss of these revenues, Murray proposed new funding sources. He suggested a graduated income tax and a sales tax on luxuries, such as cosmetics and cigarettes. The legislature did not accept his proposals, and substituted a 1 percent general sales tax, which provided considerable revenue.

While working to revise Oklahoma's tax base, Governor Murray faced the oil crisis of 1931 with unconventional methods that brought him national recognition. The oil problem developed when production vastly exceeded comsumption and the price per barrel dwindled to eighteen cents. As a result, the state's revenues, largely dependent on the oil gross production tax, declined radically. In addition, independent oil operators and stripper well owners faced bankruptcy. In August, 1931, Murray closed 3,108 prorated oil wells and called out the Oklahoma National Guard to enforce his decision. The action brought dramatic economic results. After sixty-five days, oil was at eighty-five cents per barrel, and the governor cancelled his order. In January, 1932, oil sold at one dollar per barrel. Later, in 1933, when companies violated the proration law in the Oklahoma City Oil Field, Murray closed their operations, and at once the legislature passed a bill levying severe fines for proration violations and imposing rigid enforcement.

The use of the Oklahoma National Guard by Governor Murray in the oil crisis of 1931 commenced a pattern during his administration, for he called it into state service thirty-four times. Although some occasions justified its call, others did not.

Cicero Murray, brother of Governor William H. Murray, stands at the head of a unit of Oklahoma National Guard troops ordered by the governor to enforce the shutdown of prorated oil wells in Oklahoma in 1931 (Oklahoma Publishing Company).

Murray likely enjoyed his executive authority, and the use of the national guard exemplified this power. Perhaps also its use symbolized his desire for action and change. Typical of this was his employment of the national guard in the so-called Bridge War involving the opening of a free bridge over the Red River at Denison, Texas, in opposition to a nearby toll bridge under contract with the state of Texas.

Soon the flamboyant Murray became a favorite of journalists and garnered many features stories in national magazines. His picture appeared on the cover of *Time Magazine* less than a week after he formally announced his candidacy for the presidency of the United States in February, 1932. His electioneering took him to many states and became known as the Bread, Butter, Bacon, and Beans Campaign. His platform provided for unemployment relief, old age insurance, extension of credit, revised protection tariff laws, more foreign commerce, and the reduction of international armaments. At the Democratic National Convention, Murray received twenty-three votes on the first ballot. Twenty-two were those of the Oklahoma delegation and one other was cast by his brother, a delegate from North Dakota.

Back in Oklahoma, the Great Depression continued to be Murray's major problem. He worked vigorously to fulfill his inaugural pledge that the poor and unemployed would receive care. Because of his urging, Oklahoma became the first state to appropriate money for the needy. These funds soon proved inadequate, and next Murray unsuccessfully promoted a bill levying an emergency tax on public employees for relief of the poor. He even gave part of his own salary to aid the needy. He sharply opposed the practice of sending debtors to jail and took action to prevent mortagage foreclosures on farms and homes. With the New Deal in operation, general funds for direct relief and employment relief reached Oklahoma in quantity to supplement Murray's state program for the poor and unemployed.

As governor, Murray provided a unique style and quality of leadership. He not only evaluated the problems he faced but he attacked them vigorously and predicted their future. He liked work relief for the unemployed not only because it aided them but society as well. He viewed the Oklahoma Tax Commission established under his guidance as a vehicle for stabilizing state finances and as an instrument for the equitable distribution of tax levies. Although Murray proved controversial, his blunt honesty and sincere concern brought a sense of security to his constituents.

Murray's successor, Ernest Whitworth Marland (1935-1939), another Democrat, brought a background of business experience in oil production to the executive office. After establishing and

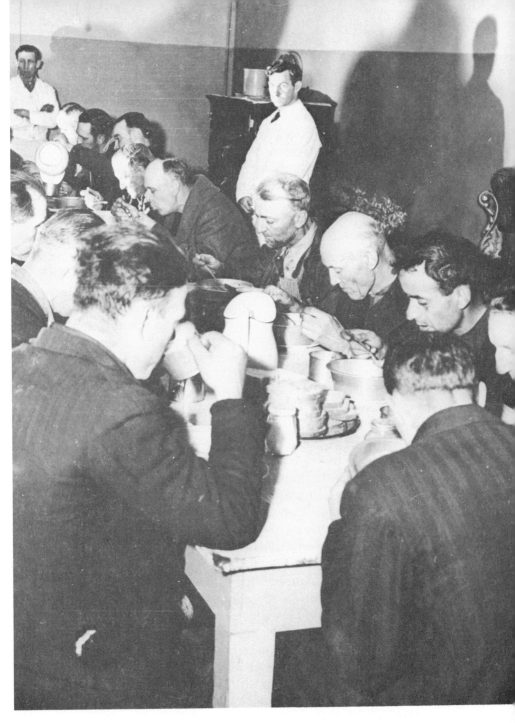

A soup line for unemployed Oklahoma citizens during the Great Depression (Oklahoma Department of Libraries).

successfully operating the Marland Oil Company, the predecessor of the Continental Oil Company, he generously shared his great wealth with his employees and Ponca City. He brought also the political experience of one term in the United States House of Representatives to his office. He believed in the New Deal and promised to apply its full impact in Oklahoma.

Like Murray, Marland chose to blunt the havoc of the Great Depression. He called on the legislature to establish state boards to deal with soil erosion, flood control, reforestation, irrigation, housing, new industries, planning, and highways. To raise the needed revenues to operate the conservation and relief efforts of the various boards, he recommended additional taxes on gasoline, oil, and natural gas. He likewise proposed tax increases on incomes, inheritances, insurance premiums, cigarettes, salaries, and rents. For relief of the poor and unemployed, he proposed a 3 percent tax on services and sales, with two-thirds of the money scheduled for relief and one-third for common schools.

Because Marland's proposals for increased taxation touched every economic interest in Oklahoma, statewide opposition developed at once. As a generous benefactor who gave away much of his large fortune, he never quite understood the intense reaction he confronted. His alarm caused him to call a joint caucus of both houses of the legislature to plead his program. Although he emphasized the need for state money to match federal funding available for relief and public work projects, he made little headway due to the fiscal conservatism of the house of representatives and its speaker, Leon C. Phillips. The speaker said the necessities of the state would be taken care of first, including a balanced budget, operating expenses, relief for those unable to work, and common school support, and then Marland's program would be considered. Thoroughly frustrated, the governor appealed to the people for their support in two statewide radio broadcasts and reminded them of their mandate to him to bring the complete national recovery program of the New Deal to Oklahoma. Opposition continued in the house of representatives and the Marland program emerged considerably reworked.

The remaining blueprint coming from the governor's first legislature consisted of but half of the proposed funds for relief, approval of the Oklahoma Planning Board and the Oklahoma Flood Control and Conservation Board with but small funding, together with additional taxes on incomes, inheritances, cigarettes, oil, sales, and services. The legislature also appropriated $8.2 million annually for common school support. Speaker Phillips largely had his way, and the governor denounced him for it.

Because Marland did not feel that the legislative relief and social security program met the needs of the state, he initiated a measure approved by the voters to provide an additional $2.5 million for relief. He continued to emphasize the need for social security legislation, a sustained taxation program, public works programs, rural redevelopment, subsistence homesteads, and enlarged state assistance for agriculture. The following year, in 1936, the voters approved an old age pension program initiated by Marland and a 2 percent sales tax to fund it.

When the legislature met in 1937, the governor decided not to present a mandated program because of his battle with the 1935 legislature. His gentle prodding brought social security legislation and generous appropriations for the next two years, but adequate funding for a balanced budget did not pass. This forced Marland to request authority to trim appropriations on a quarterly basis to meet incoming revenue, but this was denied, even with Phillips removed from the speaker's chair.

Uniquely, Marland became the first Oklahoma governor to run for the United States Senate while in office. He made the race twice and met defeat each time in the primary. Other unusual contributions include leadership in the creation and development of the Interstate Oil Compact, and the formulation of the Department of Public Safety and its highway patrol. He was also the first of several oilmen to serve as governor.

Overall, Marland's major contribution while governor consisted of winning a high degree of social security for those suffering from the Great Depression. Above all, humanitarianism motivated him, just as it had in Ponca City. He desired to use state government as the method to best serve the needs of

Federal Works Progress Administration (WPA) funds constructed asphalt roads such as this in Oklahoma during the Great Depression (Oklahoma Department of Libraries).

the economically distressed. He exerted his influence to the fullest for complete cooperation with New Deal programs so that Oklahoma would receive maximum recovery benefits. The setbacks Marland received in attempting to restore Oklahoma economically resulted from disagreement over the purpose of the state's taxation role. Yet his economic recovery efforts, although thwarted in part by the legislature, brought hope and relief to many and continued economic recovery in the state.

When Marland left office, Leon Chase Phillips (1939-1943), also a Democrat, filled the executive post. His experience included six years in the house of representatives, with two years of service as speaker. It was then that he vigorously opposed the New Deal recovery program of Governor Marland. Now that he led the state as governor he would implement further the programs that he sponsored as speaker of the house of representatives. He called for the elimination of state government extravagance, a decrease of state employees, declared his opposition to the Red River Denison Dam, then being constructed by the federal government, and maintained that the legislature should not make appropriations larger than estimated revenues. Thus the issues of his administration would be fiscal responsibility and opposition to federal programs in the state.

Like governors before him, Phillips desired for political control reasons the reorganization of the Oklahoma Highway Commission by reducing the number of commissioners by one, by granting the governor power to remove members, and by requiring the commission to operate on a cash basis. The legislature passed the bill immediately and the governor signed it into law two days after his inauguration. To balance the budget, Phillips wanted state taxes collected on time, and despite threats of his veto, the house of representatives and the senate passed a bill extending the deadline for payment of taxes and suspending all penalties and interest on unpaid taxes. The governor relented and signed the bill. Next he had a bill introduced in the legislature reducing the number of gasoline inspectors from 140 to 20. After considerable debate, the legislature agreed, and another step was taken toward a balanced budget. The legislature even cut its phone bill by $5,000, saved $15,000 on typing copies of the legislative journal, and the house of representatives reduced its employees by 25 percent. After these economies, the legislature extended the sales tax for two years, thus providing more funds for a balanced budget. The governor helped the budget again when he convinced the legislature to defeat a bill to provide free textbooks for school children.

One final source of major revenue saving did not escape the attention of Phillips, and that concerned the funding of common schools. These institutions had requested $12.8 million a year for the biennium, the same amount received for the previous two years. Phillips planned to cut the recommended appropriation to $8 million and pressure local governments to provide the additional funding. The legislature finally agreed to appropriate $11.5 million a year, an amount grudgingly acceptable to the Oklahoma Education Association. The governor also saw to it that all departments of state government cooperated in attempting to achieve a balanced budget.

The other major area of concern by Phillips revolved around federal programs in the state, and these he attacked with ethusiasm as soon as the 1939 legislature adjourned. Two federal dams under construction in Oklahoma, one on the Red River at Denison, Texas, and the other on the Grand River in Oklahoma, symbolized this intervention, according to Phillips. The Grand River Dam appeared the most vulnerable, so the governor took action against it first. When he came to office, the state government wanted $139,635 more for property that would be flooded by the dam than the federal government wished to pay. He threatened that the dam would not be completed until the state received full payment, and promised to declare martial law and call out the Oklahoma National Guard, if necessary. He said also that property of the Grand River Dam Authority could be taxed.

Then Phillips carried out his threats. In March, 1940, he declared martial law and ordered the Oklahoma National Guard to the dam. Construction could continue, but the troops had orders to prevent the closing of arch six, the only section of the dam still open. A state court then provided Phillips with a temporary restraining order preventing the closing of arch six, but a federal court next issued its own restraining order against the use of the Oklahoma National Guard to stop the completion of the dam. Soon arch six was completed and closed, and water began rising in the reservoir. The governor did not give up, left the Oklahoma National Guard at the dam, and took the problem to court. Simultaneously he threatened to fire the board of directors of the Grand River Dam Authority, and the federal government countered by threatening receivership for the authority. Phillips won momentarily when the United States Supreme Court overruled the lower federal court, but the federal government finally placed the authority in receivership for defense purposes when the United States entered World War II.

Governor Phillips saw state rights as the issue in the Red River Denison Dam. He believed that the dam would not control floods, and that Texas would mainly benefit from the power generated by the dam. Although the Oklahoma delegation in Congress supported the dam, he worked against it. He sued to prevent its construction, but the United States Supreme Court would not consider the case. After other attempts by Phillips to block the dam, settlement came when the United States entered World War II, and the dam was completed.

While Phillips fought the battle of the dams, the 1941 session of the legislature convened. The governor desired not only to continue a balanced budget, but worked toward a constitutional amendment making a balanced budget mandatory. To obtain additional revenue, he recommended new and reformed tax laws, such as an amusement tax. Other needed savings, he said, should come through reduced appropriations. Opposition to the balanced budget amendment originated generally with common school interests, who insisted that it would make the schools bear most of the burden and cause a nine month school term to be nearly impossible. With the balanced budget amendment, Phillips told teachers, a ten dollar a month pay raise would be possible because state financing would be stabilized. Regardless of common school complaints, voters approved by a two to one margin the balanced budget amendment in March, 1941, to take effect the following July.

Severe tax increases and drastic economy in state financing thus became necessary. The gasoline tax increased one and one-half cents, the cigarette tax went up two cents on a package, the tax on the gross receipts of non-state insurance companies doubled, and license tag fees went up, resulting in an extra $13 million in revenues. Virtually all state institutions received reduced appropriations. The University of Oklahoma had its annual budget reduced $800,000, Oklahoma Agricultural and Mechanical College received a cut of $400,000 annually, and governmental departments had total reductions of approximately $1 million a year. Common schools also had a cut in funds.

United States Army Air Force bombers being modified for combat in 1943 at Tinker Air Force Base, Midwest City, Oklahoma (Tinker Air Force Base).

Other significant legislation in the form of proposed constitutional amendments approved by the votes reorganized the state's institutions of higher education under one coordinating board of regents and guaranteed the payment of old-age pensions. While Phillips supported these measures, he continued to quarrel with the federal government. He attacked a proposed federal dam on the Arkansas River, he denounced Oklahoma's congressmen for permitting the state to lose more than 100,000 acres of land for the Red River Denison Dam, and protested two dams recommended by the federal government for northeastern Oklahoma.

Although Phillips regularly opposed President Roosevelt and the New Deal, he supported the federal government without exception during World War II. The day following the Pearl Harbor attack he issued a proclamation urging Oklahomans to be calm, determined, and patriotic, and cautioned citizens not to violate established justice. He announced that the state would dismiss use and sale taxes on war contracts if the federal government so desired, and he suggested using convict labor to keep war plants operating.

Under the guidance of Phillips, Oklahoma moved from deficit spending to a surplus of $5 million. His economy and budget balancing efforts won approval by the legislature and the voters, and placed Oklahoma on a permanent cash basis as the result of the budget balancing amendment of 1941. Not only did he encourage reductions in appropriations and increases in taxes to balance the state budget during his administration, but he managed to require it of future Oklahoma governors, legislators, state employees, and citizens. Only through increased tax income in the future would Oklahoma state govenment have more to spend. Although couched in state rights, the opposition of Phillips to President Roosevelt and the New Deal contained aspects of protest against federal government overspending.

Robert S. Kerr (1943-1947), another Democrat and the first native-born governor, followed Phillips in the executive office. A wealthy oilman, he had originally supported Phillips, but broke with him when Phillips repudiated President Roosevelt and the New Deal. As governor, Kerr placed top priority on retiring the state indebtedness of more than $36 million accumulated over previous administrations. He proposed strict economy and requested legislators to authorize the use of surplus funds, such as the $5 million accumulated during the Phillips administration, for debt retirement. He also opposed efforts to reduce taxes in order to preserve Oklahoma's tax base for adequate state funding and yet live within the balanced budget amendment. At the same time, he adamantly refused to support efforts to raise taxes. Together with the legislature, Kerr managed state finances so well that the entire state debt was retired by 1945.

Three constitutional amendments supported by Kerr passed the 1943 legislature and won voter approval. The Oklahoma Pardon and Parole Board resulted and consisted of a non-partisan five-member review board to examine all requests for clemency. Another amendment established a board of regents for the Oklahoma Agricultural and Mechanical College at

Victory in Japan (V-J) Day in downtown Oklahoma City, August 14, 1945, at the close of World War II (Oklahoma Publishing Company).

Stillwater and for tax-supported junior college agricultural schools in the state. A similiar amendment for the University of Oklahoma at Norman served also to keep it from political control and domination.

Kerr used the 1945 legislature to prepare for post-World War II development in Oklahoma. He reversed completely his 1943 stand on no additional taxes when he outlined legislation calling for increased spending. He wanted more money for common schools, highways, health services, and new tax incentives for individuals and industries. New revenues of about $9 million annually needed to be raised for the Kerr program. Immediately opposition arose in the legislature, but the governor used conferences and mediation to win approval, and he also spoke on statewide radio to gain public support.

Most of the new money would go to the common schools. Kerr wanted permanent state funding for their support, adequate money to upgrade the physical plants of schools, increased teacher salaries, and bus transportation for students. The legislature obliged and nearly doubled the amount of the school appropriation to $15.6 million annually for two years.

Other areas of state government received new money also. Highways received an additional $4 million each year from the federal government because the legislature passed a bill removing the allocation of money for roads from county commissioners to the Oklahoma Highway Department. Tax incentives likewise received attention, such as a community property law enabling married couples to save on federal income taxes, and other statutes exempting some types of industrial machinery from use and sales assessments. Governor Kerr then needed additional sources of revenue. He asked for a two-cent per gallon tax increase on gasoline, a new levy on automobile licenses, and a large increase in the tax on beer. The legislature agreed on Kerr's requests, and more than the needed $9 million annually poured into the state treasury.

Although Kerr's program for enlarged services and increased taxes attracted much attention, a lawsuit against thirty-three educators and textbook firms filed by Governor Phillips just before he left office also caught the imagination of the public. Phillips on behalf of the people of Oklahoma alleged that the defendants had defrauded the state of more than $5.3 million in the selection of textbooks for the public schools. The evidence against Dr. Henry G. Bennett, the president of Oklahoma Agricultural and Mechanical College and a close personal friend of Governor Kerr, appeared to be especially damaging. The petition charged Bennett with bringing out new editions of arithmetic texts authored by him without making changes from earlier volumes. Allegedly, Bennett also failed to deposit royalties from the sales of books with the William H. Murray Education Foundation, as agreed in the indenture establishing the foundation. Kerr ordered a legislative investigation of the charges in the Phillips suit as soon as he became governor. The legislative committee hesitated to act, perhaps because of possible implication, despite urging from Kerr. The legislature adjourned before the committee completed its investigations, and Kerr dropped the matter. The Phillips case went to court and during the grand jury proceedings Kerr openly supported Bennett. The judge eventually dismissed the case short of trial jury verdict by invoking the statute of limitations.

Kerr also worked for the development of Oklahoma through contacts and speeches throughout the nation. Because of his ardent support of the Democratic Party and his speaking ability, he accepted many invitations to appear before party gatherings outside of Oklahoma. He strongly supported President Roosevelt for a fourth term in 1944, and this won him the keynote speech at the Democratic National Convention. He quickly became a favorite at the White House during the Roosevelt and Truman years. He also traveled across the country on frequent occasions to boost Oklahoma as a site for new postwar industry and agricultural expansion. Although sometimes criticized for many absences from Oklahoma, he paid his own travel expenses and continued to advertise the state and the Democratic Party.

As governor, Kerr emerged as a strong and determined leader. He achieved his legislative program, enforced strict fiscal restraint, retired the state's debt, won constitutional amendments intended to remove the major state higher education institutions from political control, and mitigated the power of the governor to grant clemency through the creation of the Oklahoma Pardon and Parole Board. He not only increased the tax base of the state to balance the budget, but he also desired to use additional money for common schools, highways, and health services. Simultaneously he recognized Oklahoma's possibilities for postwar expansion and encouraged legislation to promote economic development. Kerr's Arkansas River navigation and flood control project begun during his administration opened new economic opportunities for the state and provided the springboard for his meteoric career in the United States Senate. Only the textbook scandal detracted from his administration, although his sole connection with it was to defend his long-time friend, Dr. Henry G. Bennett.

Another Democrat, Roy Joseph Turner (1947-1951), followed Kerr in the executive office. With but little formal education beyond grade school, Turner amassed a fortune as an oilman and rancher. With homes in both Oklahoma City and at his huge Hereford Heaven Ranch near Sulphur, Turner became well-known while traveling around the state. For seven years he served on the Oklahoma City School Board and spent considerable time visiting in the Oklahoma Capitol, where many enjoyed his genial personality and hospitality. With this background, he accepted the suggestion of his ranching associates that he run for governor in 1946.

After a hard and long campaign, Turner won the executive office. He asked the 1947 legislature to reorganize the Oklahoma Highway Commission, the Oklahoma Tax Commission, the Oklahoma Game and Fish Commission, and the Oklahoma Planning and Resources Board. He propose to develop agriculture and industry through centralized highways and reduced taxes. The legislature readily complied with his commission and board reorganization plans and also his highway plan. A part of the road plan turned out to be a bill passed by the legislature for the construction of the Turner Turnpike between Oklahoma City and Tulsa, but several years would pass before it became a reality. The toll road project lacked funding and faced opposition by many small towns on the proposed route. In addition, the superhighway drew opposition from the National Grange, the National Association of Motor Bus Operators, the American Farm Bureau, and the American Automobile Association.

The 1947 legislature also passed other legislation recommended by Turner. A bill to reorganize the Oklahoma Board of Education, to consolidate school districts with fewer than thirteen children, and to provide for an additional one-cent tax on gasoline for county commissioner use in building all-weather roads on school bus routes collected strong resentment in rural areas, but finally won approval. Other legislation recommended by Turner and later approved called for $2 million to finance a program for war veterans, broadened vocational rehabilitation laws, established a vocational education division, provided for training centers for crippled children, and for a new mental health law.

The first legislature during Turner's administration appropriated a total of $104 million for the biennium, an increase of $29 million allotted over the previous two years. Although higher education funds grew by $8 million for the biennium, the

Residents of Oklahoma City viewing the first television programs aired in Oklahoma, July 1, 1949 (Oklahoma Publishing Company).

amount was less than requested by the schools. State mental institutions, however, doubled their allotment over the two previous years. Even with a one-third cut in the state income tax, adequate money remained to fund Turner's program.

With the 1949 legislature, Turner faced new challenges to his desire to hold the line on taxes and still fund his program. He asked the legislature to continue with the centralized re-organization plan for school districts, to provide for major developments in mental health and public welfare, to increase salaries of common school teachers, to increase funding for free textbooks, and to provide more money for higher education. In other areas, he recommended more funding for agricultural research, for improvements in vocational training, for con-servation aid, and for improvement of recreational facilities and state parks. He also lobbied for more and better school and farm-to-market roads, and to finance these he called for a one-cent increase in the gasoline tax together with automobile and farm truck license revenue. He vigorously fought the stubborn opposition of the Oklahoma County Commissioners Association to give road maintenance and construction priority to secondary roads, and not to the school and farm-to-market roads.

A group of dignitaries visit at the Oklahoma City gate of the Turner Turnpike a few days before the opening of the toll road in May of 1953 (Oklahoma Turnpike Authority).

Although Turner did not find the 1949 legislature as responsive to his programs as the 1947 legislature, he still had some success. His free textbook pledge won support in the public school bill consisting of $50 million from the total appropriated amount of $142.5 million for the biennium. The legislature, nevertheless, wholly rejected his plea for more consolidation of school districts and his recommendation for their taxation support. Mental health and higher education institutions received increased money, but not to the extent requested. The Oklahoma Crippled Children's Commission won approval, an integrated state purchasing system received sanction, and a classified system for prisoners in penal institution went into effect.

Perhaps Turner's major achievement came in highways. The legislature followed his advice by removing $13 million from the general fund for highway use and by placing the direction of the farm-to-market road program under the Oklahoma Highway Department. The legislature also approved his recommendations against overloaded trucks and enforced speed limits on state highways. Another Turner victory for highways came with the revival of the Turner Turnpike in the 1949 legislature. Although faced with much opposition, Turner convinced the legislature that the project would be successful. With renewed legislation for the turnpike, financing came from revenue bonds purchased by out-of-state business interests, and during the last year of Turner's term, construction began. The new superhighway ranked as the third experiment of its kind west of the Mississippi River.

Although Turner probably traveled less than Kerr outside of Oklahoma, he managed to make numerous trips to Washington, D. C., where he went to bargain for federal grants to help his road programs. His prestige grew as a result of these conferences with high-level government officials, usually in the company of Harry W. "Coach" McNeil of Oklahoma City. He grew in special favor with President Harry S. Truman when Truman's campaign train entered Oklahoma in 1948 lacking funds. Through private contributions, Turner raised all the money the president needed to campaign in Oklahoma. Truman responded with a personal letter thanking Turner for his generous service during the campaign. The president was so impressed with Turner that he named him national chairman of the Truman-Barkley for President Club. After reelection, Truman invited Turner to become secretary of agriculture, but the governor declined because he wanted to complete his term of office.

Turner worked to maximize the efficiency of state bureaucracy through the consolidation and update of state agencies and through an improved transportation network. His administration made strides in consolidating and improving the quality of rural school education, and in general helped farmers make the conversion to mechanized agriculture. He launched the turnpike system of Oklahoma. The Turner Turnpike proved to be the beginning of the largest state toll road network west of the Mississippi River. Turner always had his eyes on the unfortunate people of Oklahoma, and these he assisted through enlarged vocational education and rehabilitation programs, training centers for crippled children, and a new mental health law. In other areas, he achieved funding for the state's free textbook system and won a classified method for prisoners in penal institutions. Through growth in industry and agriculture, adequate money came to the state to fund Turner's programs and make possible a one-third cut in state income tax.

Yet another Democrat, Johnston Murray (1951-1955), followed Turner as governor. Murray came to the office exactly twenty years after his father, William H. Murray, and brought some of his characteristics, but few of his political insights. William H. Murray knew how to maintain his political viability, but Johnston did not. Like his father, he believed in personal education, and to better prepare himself for work he completed the law degree at Oklahoma City University at about forty-five years of age. Like Turner, he had little political preparation for the executive office, although he had served the Democratic Party on the local level and worked for the state as chairman of the Oklahoma Election Board and as secretary of the Oklahoma Land Commission. His father was both an asset and a liability when he decided to run for governor. The elder Murray aroused the Democratic Party in Oklahoma when he refused to support President Franklin D. Roosevelt for reelection in 1936. On the other hand, the magic of the Murray name still had great drawing power among state voters, and Johnston made much of this in his successful "Just Plain Folks" campaign in which he emphasized economy in government and no new taxes.

When the 1951 legislature met, in keeping with the anti-communism program throughout the nation, it passed a bill requiring all state employees to take a loyalty oath denying support of communism and certifying willingness to take up arms in defense of the United States. Murray agreed with the bill and signed it, although it was eventually declared unconstitutional by the United States Supreme Court. It was then replaced by a similar bill in the 1953 legislature, also signed by Murray. It has not been declared unconstitutional.

Two major proposals important to Murray came up for consideration in the 1951 legislature. First, he proposed to raise and equalize the assessment of property values statewide. His plan called for increasing property assessments to 35 percent of their actual value and contained provisions for the Oklahoma Tax Commission to penalize counties refusing to comply with the law by withholding state money. Through this system, the state could raise more funds at the local level for the support of education, thereby freeing additional funds for other state uses. Second, Murray would exempt new industry coming to Oklahoma from ad valorem taxes on property and user taxes on equipment for five years. This legislation would encourage new industry to locate in Oklahoma, a promise of Murray during his campaign. The legislature failed to pass the bill intended to raise and equalize property taxes, and passed a weaker version of the bill planned to exempt new industry from ad valorem taxes on property and user taxes on equipment. Meanwhile, Murray yielded on his no-new-tax stand when he signed a bill placing a tax on beer.

Then major opposition came when the house of representatives approved a resolution providing that the legislature would recess instead of adjourning at the end of the legislative session. This resolution meant that only the legislature could call itself into session through its leaders or a majority of the members of each chamber. If this resolution had passed the senate, the governor could not have called special sessions of the legislature. Evidently Murray failed to give direction to his proposed legislature through lack of conferences with legislative leaders and adequate emphasis on his program. The legislature sailed through its remaining appropriation business without obvious direction from Murray except for his bill to establish the Governor's Joint Committee on Reorganization of State Government. It passed without evident opposition, although overall the Murray program had failed.

When the 1953 legislature met, Murray once again came up with a meager program. He continued his campaign stand on economy in government and no new taxes. In addition, he repeated most of his previous program. He encouraged the legislators to economize by consolidating boards and commissions, eliminating unnecessary agencies, doing away with lump-sum appropriations whenever possible, and by checking budget requests by an agency other than the one using the requested funds. He asked as in 1951 that ad valorem property taxes be equalized, that the Governor's Joint Committee on

Reorganization of State Government be extended at least two years, and that earmarked funds be eliminated. Likely the most controversial recommendation of Murray to the legislature concerned his plan to consolidate some of Oklahoma's counties. He had brought himself to the point of believing that county reduction was inevitable due to ineffectual government in some counties and improved transportation that obviated the need for so many county governments.

Soon the legislature reacted adversely to the Murray program. A resolution passed by the house of representatives told Murray that his message called for no further explanation and that the house of representatives would reform the government as necessary to bring greater economy and efficiency. The house of representatives then passed still another resolution aimed at the governor when it established the Governmental Reform Committee selected by the house of representatives leadership. This resolution prohibited the committee from studying the governor's recommendation to consolidate the counties of the state. Ineffective leadership again caused Murray to fail with the legislature. To redeem himself, he resorted to vetoing bills, as he had with his first legislature. But with his second legislature, for the first time since the Marland administration, he had vetoes annulled again and again.

The governor and the legislature finally agreed on an enlarged highway program, an expansion of the Oklahoma Turnpike Authority, a proposed extension of the Turner Turnpike from Tulsa to the Missouri line, and legislation making a north-south turnpike possible from the Texas line to the Kansas border. Progress came also in agreement on an enlarged mental health program and the establishment of the Oklahoma Educational Television Authority.

After the legislature adjourned, Murray's disgust with its members increased, and he denounced them in a speech as being "completely gutless" for not ceasing to earmark funds. Soon the *Saturday Evening Post* contacted him to write a highly critical article about the state, and it appeared several months after Murray left office under the title "Oklahoma is in a Mess!" Purporting to be an expose of how greed and poor government had retarded the state, Murray saw the drop in state population as the result of the lack of jobs which could be solved by attracting new industry. He viewed taxation in Oklahoma as oppressive and the legislature as obsolete in its attitudes and procedures. He described the lack of a merit system for state employees, criticized the long ballot, castigated overproduction in oil, and labeled county commissioners as generally corrupt. In concluding, Murray described Oklahoma as "at least a generation behind the times."

Murray lacked an adequate understanding of human relations, an attribute that plagued him throughout his years as governor. When he should have worked closely with the legislature to sell his program, he remained aloof, thus conveying the impression that he was insincere and shallow. Undeniably, Murray lost control of the legislature because of his ineffective leadership. He appeared incapable of doing more than voicing his program in formal presentations. He seemed not to have the personality and judgment for the executive office to which he was elected. Yet his "Oklahoma is in a Mess!" article presaged a number of reforms that came to the state's economy and government in the years ahead.

Oklahoma's governors from 1929 to 1955 shared many common concerns and patterns, but also some differences. All were Democrats politically, all were fiscally conservative except Marland and Kerr, and all worked well with the legislature except Johnston Murray. Only two of the governors, William H. Murray and Phillips, used the Oklahoma National Guard to a considerable extent. Holloway, Phillips, and Turner wanted the Oklahoma Highway Commission reorganized, likely because of legislative and patronage pressures. Holloway bridged the executive office from the prosperity of the 1920s to the Great Depression of the 1930s. Then Murray, Marland, and Phillips worked effectively to take Oklahoma through the New Deal years of the Great Depression to the prosperity of World War II. With Kerr in the executive office, he began a vigorous trend to bring new industry to the state. Then Turner and Johnston Murray carried on this thrust with equal enthusiasm.

In some cases, patterns appeared in a variety of legislation sponsored by Oklahoma's chief executives between 1929 and 1955. Holloway in 1929 first promoted a constitutional amendment creating separate boards of regents for the agricultural and mechanical colleges and the University of Oklahoma, only to have it passed by the legislature and then defeated by the voters; Kerr proposed similar amendments in 1943 that won approval by both the legislature and the voters. Holloway first proposed the Oklahoma Tax Commission, and under the next governor, William H. Murray, another bill established it immediately. With but a meager beginning under Henry S. Johnston, Holloway's immediate predecessor, the use of general revenue funds to assist in the support of common schools commenced and continued with regular increases urged by all the governors except Phillips and Johnston Murray. Each of the governors promoted increases in expenditures for the state highway system, and Turner worked untiringly to build the turnpike between Oklahoma City and Tulsa that bears his name. Johnston Murray took up the cudgel for additional turnpike construction, and eventually the system developed into the most extensive west to the Mississippi River. In the area of mental health, special emphasis began under Kerr, and continued unabated during the administrations of Turner and Johnston Murray.

Perhaps the single most notable achievement by any governor during the years from 1929 to 1955 came from Phillips in the form of the balanced budget amendment to the constitution. For years the state budget remained unbalanced, and slowly but surely the state debt increased. Phillips decided this must change, and he first worked toward this end while serving as speaker of the house of representatives during the first two years of the Marland administration. When he followed Marland in the executive office, he succeeded in maintaining a balanced budget in his first biennial legislature, and then in his second biennial legislature in 1941 he successfully promoted a balanced budget amendment. It also won approval by the voters. Not only did Phillips demand and achieve a balanced budget during his administration, but he managed also to require it of future Oklahoma governors, legislators, state employees, and citizens.

William Judson Holloway

Governor of Oklahoma, 1929-1931

By Maynard J. Hanson

William Judson Holloway

Before all of Oklahoma's senators had voted at the conclusion of Governor Henry S. Johnston's impeachment trial, it became apparent the Oklahoma Senate would remove him from office on the afternoon of March 20, 1929. Senators who had already voted and other interested bystanders rushed through the halls of the capitol building to the fourth floor lieutenant governor's office. Eager to congratulate Johnston's successor, the noisy crowd of well-wishers discovered the lieutenant governor was at his home, and his secretary, Eva Mae Hodges, telephoned William Judson Holloway to inform him that he had become the governor of Oklahoma.

While awaiting Holloway's arrival, the crowd maintained its enthusiasm. They congratulated Representative H. Tom Kight for his prosecution summation urging Johnston's removal; he replied that the speech had exhausted him. Others examined tally lists to determine how each senator had voted on the impeachment charges. Holloway's appearance satisifed the well-wishers and brought order to the crowded room. After arranging chairs for women visitors and establishing a receiving line for new arrivals, he conferred with Oklahoma National

Guard Adjutant General Charles F. Barrett about arrangements for the oath of office. Chief Justice Charles W. Mason, who had presided over Johnston's trial and who would soon confront his own impeachment, arrived and administered the oath of office in a simple ceremony.[1]

After the turmoil and tension associated with the impeachment process of the previous weeks, the friendly greetings Holloway extended to visitors of all political persuasions must have been reassuring. The new governor attempted to convey the same message to all of the state's residents and issued a statement: "The best interests and the happiness and prosperity of the average citizen of Oklahoma is now and must remain the paramount issue. An era of good will must be brought about among the people of our state."[2] In a time of governmental paralysis, Holloway's confident manner, assurances of governmental restoration, and previous career in government dispelled thoughts of continued political disintegration in Oklahoma.

Holloway's early career provided him with sound preparation for the governorship. The only son of Stephen Lee and Molly Horne Holloway, he was born on December 15, 1888, in Arkadelphia, Arkansas. His mother died in 1892, and his father, who later remarried, established a successful ministerial career in Arkansas, Oklahoma, and Texas Baptist churches. Young Holloway started his academic career at his father's alma mater, Ouachita College in Arkadelphia, and established a lifelong friendship with an older Ouachita College student, Henry G. Bennett, when he stayed at a boarding house operated by Bennett's parents. Holloway received a bachelor of arts degree in the spring of 1910 and studied at the University of Chicago the following summer.

Through Bennett's influence, Holloway obtained an appointment as elementary school principal at Hugo, Oklahoma, in the fall of 1910. When Bennett received a promotion to the superintendency of the Hugo schools, he promoted Holloway to high school principal. While working as principal, Holloway began reading law at night.

Holloway left Hugo in the fall of 1914 and attended Cumberland University in Lebanon, Tennessee. He returned to Hugo the next year with a bachelor of laws degree, gained admittance to the state bar, and started a private law practice. Hugo's new attorney discovered that establishing a law practice could be financially unrewarding and accepted the Democratic nomination for prosecuting attorney in Choctaw County. His election to that office in 1916 launched his political career.

Not all of Holloway's time in Hugo involved law and politics, however. Soon after beginning his law practice, he met another Ouachita College graduate at an evening social gathering. Amy Arnold, born on September 30, 1894, was the daughter of Richard W. and Fannie (Nuckolls) Arnold of Texarkana, Arkansas, and had been hired by Bennett as a school teacher. She married Holloway in Texarkana on June 16, 1917, and they established a home in Hugo. Unfortunately, United States involment in World War I disrupted their lives. Holloway volunteered for officers' school and trained near Louisville, Kentucky, at Camp Zachary Taylor during October and November, 1918, but the war ended before he could be sent overseas.[3]

In 1920, Holloway entered and won the state senatorial campaign for the twenty-fourth district of Choctaw, McCurtain, and Pushmataha counties. Among his colleagues, he earned a reputation as an affable and energetic legislator. In his home district, Holloway also maintained his popularity. When he sought a second senatorial term in 1924, he won the election without opposition.

As a freshman senator, Holloway's legislative work brought him into contact with Mrs. Lamar Looney, a Democrat from Hollis and Oklahoma's first female state senator. In a speech delivered on the floor of the senate, he told his colleagues that he had been raised to believe that women did not belong in politics, and although he would not admit it in his senatorial campaign, he still had held those beliefs when he entered the senate. His association with Senator Looney changed his opinion and led him to praise her work.[4] Concerning the future of women in politics, Holloway remarked: "If the other women of this state exercise the same splendid judgment in public affairs that Senator Looney has, I say to you that I hope her tribe will increase."[5]

Holloway's second senatorial term brought him closer to the center of political affairs in Oklahoma. When the position of president pro tempore of the senate became vacant after the 1924 elections, the opening disrupted the line of succession to the governor's office. Lieutenant Governor Martin E. Trapp had become governor after the impeachment of Governor John C. Walton in 1923. Without a lieutenant governor or president pro tempore to serve as acting governor in his absence, Governor Trapp called a special session of the senate in November and instructed them to elect a new presiding officer. They selected Holloway by unanimous vote.[6]

During Trapp's administration, Holloway served as acting governor several times. On issues that could wait until Trapp's return, he deferred exercising his authority, but at the suggestion of an appeals court, he granted one man a reprieve from execution. In search of a story on these occasions, reporters often found Oklahoma's acting governor weeding his garden.[7]

These years marked continued growth in Holloway's popularity. He maintained personal and correspondence contacts with various people around the state and helped others, Henry G. Bennett among them, obtain railroad passes. Political rumor established him as a gubernatorial candidate for the next election, and his Choctaw County friends judged the governor's race as a viable proposition.[8]

Apparently, Holloway considered another office more attainable. In the summer of 1926, he entered the campaign for the Democratic nomination as lieutenant governor. Stephen Holloway, a half brother, and Arnold Moseley, Amy's nephew, contributed to the campaign by making contacts and erecting signs in eastern Oklahoma. Against twelve others, Holloway collected 74,529 votes; his nearest competitor received 29,386 votes. An uneventful campaign against the Republican candidate, W. S. Caldwell of Pawnee, followed, and Holloway won the November election by a margin of 197,783 votes to 155,834 votes. Holloway, along with a complete slate of Democratic winners headed by gubernatorial candidate Henry S. Johnston, took office in January, 1927.[9]

Despite the Democrats' success at the ballot box, party unity dissipated. Johnston's relations with the legislature became a disastrous squabble. His handling of highway affairs, patronage, and pardons, his confidential secretary's penchant for restricting access to him, and his alleged incompetency in office served as sources of complaint against him. In 1927, he thwarted impeachment plans by using the Oklahoma National Guard to disperse an illegally assembled session of the legislature, but he failed to avoid impeachment in the regular session of 1929.[10]

Throughout this political turbulence, Holloway maintained a neutral position and helped engineer a major appointment in the state. The president of Oklahoma Agricultural and Mechanical College at Stillwater, Bradford Knapp, resigned in 1928. The institution's alumni association preferred selecting a new president from a group of nationally recognized educators, but the Oklahoma Board of Agriculture controlled the college's affairs. The board's president, Harry B. Cordell, and Holloway were close friends. With Holloway's sponsorship, Henry G. Bennett, who had advanced to the presidency of Southeastern State Teachers College in Durant, became the board's choice. The selection elicited some criticism, but Cordell defended the board's action.[11]

Holloway's unobtrusive position as lieutenant governor finally changed on January 21, 1929. The senate approved articles of impeachment against Johnston and suspended him from office. Until the outcome of the impeachment trial became known, their action elevated Holloway to acting governor. Holloway avoided gestures interpretable as favoritism, handled routine matters only, deferred issuing pardons, and persuaded the Oklahoma Highway Commission to delay a large bid letting. When the senate finally removed Johnston for incompetency, Holloway derived benefits from his diplomatic stance. Neither Johnston's friends nor Johnston's enemies resented the new governor.[12]

Within the state and across the nation, the impeachment had tarnished Oklahoma's image and had stigmatized the office of governor. Citing Oklahoma's frequent impeachments as proof, numerous national newspaper editors suggested that the state

had been granted statehood too early.[13] Holloway recognized
the problem and made an attempt to return the people of the
state to what he called "solid thinking."[14] As part of this effort,
Holloway told members of the Oklahoma City Gibbons Club:
"My sole ambition is to serve honorably and efficiently; my hope
is that at the end of two years I still will have my self-respect."[15]

A natural and generous personality aided the governor's
restoration program. In contrast to Johnston's administration,
visitors crowded Holloway's office, and each left with the
impression he had received the governor's complete attention.
Holloway's concern for image even extended to photographic
poses. He habitually drew one foot onto the seat of his chair
during conversation. When a photographer requested a picture
in this position, he believed the pose was undignified and
declined the request.[16] Oklahoma's first lady presented a similar
image. Amy Holloway revealed that she bought her husband's
clothes ready-made and that they liked to read for recreation,
but not too much. When asked if their newly acquired position
might change them, she replied: "We are just the same today as
yesterday, and we'll be the same tomorrow."[17]

Holloway's first involvement in state affairs concerned the
legislature. With most of its attention directed towards
investigation and impeachment, the legislature had accomplished little. The governor requested the passage of a highway
bill abolishing the five highway commissioners, a source of
dissatisfaction under Johnston, and the creation of a new three-
member commission. Because he had not had time to formulate
a constructive legislative program, he asked that the legislators
adjourn and promised to recall them. They complied with both
requests.[18]

In addition to the new highway commissioners, other
bureaucratic vacancies allowed Holloway to make a number of
appointments, but low salaries hampered his search for qualified
personnel. After offering one position to five prospective
candidates and failing to fill it, he remarked: "We are not going
to offer it to just any Tom, Dick and Harry. . . . We will let it go
vacant if we can't get someone that we feel is competent to do
the work."[19] Other prospective appointees, such as *Altus Times-
Democrat* editor Hutton Bellah who refused an offer to become

Louis (Lew) Wentz, oilman and philanthropist of Ponca City, was selected by Governor Holloway to serve as chairman of the Oklahoma Highway Commission (Western History Collections, University of Oklahoma Library).

the governor's private secretary, claimed that they did not have time for governmental service. Walter A. Hadley, a Stroud businessman, accepted and broke a tradition of journalists holding the private secretary's position.[20] By not meeting Holloway's standards, applicants recommended by legislators did not simplify his search, and he told the politicans: "You may help make appointments for jobs at the capitol, but these appointees will get their walking papers unless they are thoroughly capable of holding their jobs."[21]

When selecting the chairman of the Oklahoma Highway Commission, the governor's insistence upon outstanding officials induced him to take an unusual action. The new highway bill had created a six-year term for the chairman, and it was a major governmental position. Holloway's choice was Louis (Lew) Haynes Wentz of Ponca City. Oilman, millionaire, philanthropist, and possible canidate for the Republican gubernatorial nomination, Wentz feared the chairmanship might interfere with his business affairs. Republicans believed they might lose a good candidate; Democrats thought they might create a viable candidate. Nobody questioned his business acumen, however, and Wentz's wealth helped place him above suspicion in an office susceptible to corruption. The governor asked Oklahoma's citizens and newspapers to urge the millionaire to accept the job. Wentz relented in early April, 1929,

Unbearably dusty when dry and nearly impassable when wet, the old Williams Highway east of Valliant in McCurtain County was typical of Oklahoma's unimproved roads (Oklahoma Historical Society).

and Holloway escorted him arm in arm on a tour of the highway department offices after the swearing in ceremony.[22] The occasion prompted Holloway to comment: "The acceptance of Wentz makes me the happiest governor in the United States."[23]

As in the rest of the nation, Oklahoma highway maintenance and construction had become a major govermental service and concern that accentuated Wentz's appointment. Between 1924 and 1929, Oklahoma's highway system had increased from 4,523 miles to 6,289 miles, but approximately three-fourths of the system remained unpaved. Motor vehicles on Oklahoma roads had nearly doubled during the same period to 602,000. The highway department had more than 2,500 employees and a budget in excess of $16 million. When Holloway completed the commission appointments with two Democrats, Durant banker and wholesale grocer Samuel C. Boswell and Chickasha cotton mill operator L. C. Hutson, he believed he had placed the department under capable supervision.[24]

The completion of these appointments allowed the governor to turn his attention toward the upcoming special session of the legislature, and the state's budget required extra attention. The regular legislative session had adjourned without adopting an appropriations bill for the fiscal year that would begin on July 1, 1929, and the state also had incurred a deficit during the past fiscal year. The debt had forced Holloway to veto reluctantly a $500,000 school aid bill during the regular session, but nearly a $2 million liability remained. Without waiting for the Oklahoma Equalization Board to establish revenue levels, he made his own revenue projections. To prevent the legislature from making excessive appropriations, he worked closely with Senator Tom Anglin and Representative H. Tom Kight, chairmen of their respective appropriations committees. Their work resulted in a biennial budget of $29 million for departmental and institutional services and allowed another $2 million for elimination of the current debt.[25]

On May 16, 1929, Holloway convened the special legislative session and revealed his legislative program before a joint meeting of senators and representatives. After telling them that his office did not have sufficient funds to prepare copies of his message, he strongly emphasized the restrictions on the budget and threatened to veto excessive appropiations. The remainder of the governor's speech called for reforms and improvements in various departments and institutions.[26]

Highway affairs were a major concern of the administration and constituted an important part of Holloway's legislative program. Toll bridges across several Oklahoma rivers had been an issue in the 1928 political campaigns, and the governor urged their abolition. Passage of a toll bridge and toll road law, introduced in the house of representatives, allowed the highway commission to condemn and purchase such structures, build free bridges as alternatives, and cooperate with the state of Texas when necessary. A companion bill in the senate ended the franchise authority of toll corporations. Implementation of these laws resulted in considerable litigation, all decided in the state's favor, and required passage of a federal law permitting Texas and Oklahoma to cooperate in building and operating bridges across the Red River.[27]

Although the house of representatives had adopted the toll bridge bill by a ninety-one to one margin, another proposal failed to create equal enthusiasm. Holloway had discerned that sentiment existed for a bond issue that would be used to pave completely the state highway system, and he appointed a committee of bankers to assist in drafting the details of the $150 million bond issue. As introduced in the house of representatives, the measure was a constitutional amendment creating a bond authority, but it also increased highway commissioner terms to six years. The six year terms created a partisan split in the house of representatives; Republicans feared complete Democratic control of the highway commission.[28]

Two days before the representatives voted on the bill, Holloway tried to save it from defeat. In a special message to the representatives, he said: "The demand for good roads in Oklahoma comes from every section and every county within our borders. They are expecting the Legislature to find the best solution and the best plan, and it takes no prophet to know that they want it done now." In addition, he expressed confidence in the highway commissioners he had appointed and claimed: "They themselves are above petty considerations of any kind; partisan bias will never enter into the consideration of their public duties."[29] The night before the scheduled vote, Oklahoma Highway Commission Chairman Lew Wentz gave a banquet at the Skirvin Hotel for the Republicans and approved their opposition to the bond issue. The next day, June 28, 1929, the bill failed to receive the required majority.[30]

The governor's education program encountered less opposition. He told the legislature: "The institutions of higher education in Oklahoma have grown up like mushrooms overnight, every institution with its own separate board; every one in its own sphere; no co-relation with the institution over yonder or yonder or yonder." A permanent solution to the problem could not be found, he said, until the state "assumes

The Oklahoma Auto Club and the Oklahoma City Police Department sponsored a vehicle safety inspection program in September, 1930. Governor Holloway is shown having his car inspected first. It received an "OK" sticker (Oklahoma Publishing Company).

responsibility for determining an intelligent plan for the future development of its colleges."[31]

The "intelligent plan" required constitutional amendments and new laws. The Oklahoma Board of Agriculture controlled all agricultural and mechanical colleges, but the board was susceptible to political pressure. At one time, there had been three different boards appointed in one month, and the Oklahoma Agricultural and Mechanical College had three presidents in one year. The University of Oklahoma had a similar problem; its board of regents served at the pleasure of the legislature. Holloway's solution, which the legislature accepted, was a constitutional amendment establishing separate boards of regents for the University of Oklahoma and for the agricultural and mechanical colleges. When submitted to a vote of the people in the November, 1930, elections, the amendments did not receive the necessary majority.

Holloway believed that schools not under the jurisdiction of these two boards could be governed by the Oklahoma Board of Education. A senate bill transferring control of several schools to the board failed in the house of representatives. Another bill, designed to end duplication of programs between schools, passed and created a coordinating board of various college administrators. Holloway never appointed its two public members, and the superintendent of public instruction never called it into session.[32]

Reforms for common schools also received a varied reception. The 1925 legislature had created a textbook commission, but it only adopted textbooks every five years and made the governor a member of the commission. Holloway asked for a permanent commission, a staggered system of textbook adoption, a technically qualified commission, and the removal of the governor from the commission. Holloway argued: "Now, what in the world would I know about adopting textbooks, and what I say about myself applies to every other Governor that ever sat in the Governor's Office in Oklahoma."[33] Holloway also requested centralized certification of teachers by the Oklahoma Board of Education. Local boards of education had certified teachers, and the procedure created confusion. The legislature enacted both suggestions into law.[34]

Financing common schools was a more perplexing problem. Many school districts had reached the limit of their taxing authority and could not maintain an eight-month school term. The 1927 legislature began aiding these "weak schools" by direct appropriations from general revenues, but the aid was usually inadequate. Although the 1929 legislature increased school aid by $250,000, neither the state nor the local district could maintain quality education.

Holloway preferred a different approach to the problem and asked for tax reform. He proposed creation of a tax commission to equalize assessments, uncover tax evasion, and evaluate alternative revenue systems. Senators representing large corporations bitterly opposed a tax commission. The legislators refused to act, and Holloway never pressured them.[35]

On July 5, 1929, the legislature adjourned amidst charges of bribery and drunkenness. Representative Joe Sherman, a Major County Republican, alleged that representatives had received bribes to defeat bills and that senators were drunk while Holloway addressed them. His charges nearly started a fist fight and provided a wild ending to a constructive legislative session.[36]

Despite the failure of the highway bond issue and the tax commission, Holloway considered his legislative program a success. Besides the highway and education measures, the legislature had approved increased salaries for state officials and a runoff primary.[37] Now that the session had ended, Holloway observed: "There has been a feeling that when the legislature adjourned and you members are back home, hell will break loose and this department will go helter-skelter. It will not make any difference in my conduct whether you are in session or not."[38]

In addition to politics, other problems confronted Holloway and remained throughout his term of office. On the same day that Oklahomans read in the newspaper about Admiral Richard E. Byrd's exploits in Antarctica and aviator Charles Lindbergh and Anne Morrow's wedding, Oklahoma wheat prices dropped below one dollar per bushel for the first time in fifteen years. The state's economy weakened after the national stock market crash in October, 1929, and a downward trend in petroleum prices damaged another major Oklahoma industry. The unemployed patronized Oklahoma City's first bread lines in January, 1930, and one of the worst blizzards in history covered the state in the same month.[39]

Governor Holloway blamed the economic depression on factors beyond the state's control: overproduction, speculation, and high tariffs. He attempted, however, to use the resources of goverment to alleviate its effects. A drought relief commission secured a grant from the federal government to purchase seed for farmers. The Oklahoma School Land Office changed its investment procedures and invested surplus revenues in farm land instead of bonds. Weak and inefficient banks received encouragement to liquidate or to consolidate with stronger institutions. The Oklahoma Highway Department, benefitting from a one cent per gallon fuel tax increase and additional federal funds, let as many contracts as possible in an attempt to create jobs. Reduced revenues wrecked the state's budget and forced a reduction in spending by other departments, and they could not create additional jobs.[40]

Reduced revenues required administrative creativity to implement new programs. The financing of common schools needed studying, and Holloway persuaded twenty-one citizens to serve without pay on a special commission to consider the problem. To finance the inquiry, the commission raised its own funds. Another special commission served without pay, at the governor's request, and became Oklahoma's first pardon and parole board.[41]

Not all aspects of the governorship involved state affairs, however. The Holloways invited their relatives to spend the Christmas of 1929 in the governor's mansion, and eighteen of them filled its rooms on Christmas Eve. The large family gathering was a memorable event for the Holloways, and nearly forty years later, the governor reminisced for a reporter: "It seemed like home rather than a mansion. It was an unusual experience for the family on both sides. Christmas afternoon was a lesson in Oklahoma history. We drove around town and visited the capitol."[42]

The Christmas interlude ended, and the new year brought a return to politics. On January 3, 1930, Lew Wentz, during a highway commission meeting, charged that Ed McDonald, secretary of the highway department, was incompetent and suggested that the highway commission should replace him. Commissioners Hutson and Boswell defended McDonald against the chairman's attack, but they could not stop Wentz from making more charges.[43]

One week later, Wentz announced that he would no longer sign pay vouchers for McDonald's department and cited the improper behavior of one of McDonald's employees, Ed Andruss, as proof of McDonald's incompetency. Andruss had audited motor vehicle license agents during November and December, 1929, but McDonald had fired him when he learned that Andruss had been making political evaluations of the counties he visited. Wentz implied that Holloway had arranged the job for Andruss, that McDonald had instructed Andruss to make the reports, and that the reports had been given to Holloway.

Wentz's allegations, political speculators indicated, would cause Holloway to fire him, but the governor chose another course.[44] He issued a press release which stated: "I was amazed and disappointed when . . . there appeared in the public press of our state an open attack on his two colleagues on the commission and in addition thereto a vicious imputation against the integrity of the governor of the state." Holloway also asserted that Wentz had taken a partisan approach and had disclosed a narrow and unfair view, but the governor said: "I shall for the moment pursue a course of watchful waiting, still hoping that Mr. Wentz may adopt a broader view and that roads and road building will be uppermost in his mind."[45] In Wentz's defense, the *Ponca City News* editorialized: "Holloway's public attack on Chairman Wentz has revealed to the state the true man. From him has fallen the cloak of honest administration. . . . Before the bar of public opinion you must answer for your actions."[46]

Although it was a biased editorial, it contained an element of truth. Holloway had to consider public opinion, for he was the leading candidate for the Democratic nomination in the United States senatorial campaign. On January 19, 1930, Holloway

called the first Sunday press conference since the administration
of Governor John C. Walton in 1923 and created the biggest
political story since Johnston's impeachment. He announced he
would not seek the senatorial nomination. Holloway cited
neglect of gubernatorial duties during a campaign and party
welfare as reasons. His statement concluded: "I am profoundly
grateful for the high honors already conferred upon me by
fellow citizens. I am happy to submerge my personal ambitions
and fortunes, and do that which seems best for the welfare of
my state and my party."[47]

Although not mentioned at the press conference, personal
finances entered into Holloway's decision. He had discovered
that the governor's salary was inadequate and had informed the
legislature of this in 1929.[48] In later years, Holloway told a
reporter: "Public life is fine for people who can financially afford
it, but there comes a time for people with average means to get
back into their chosen work and accomplish something there. I
made up my mind to devote myself to my family and the practice
of law, and it worked out very well."[49]

Political speculation interpreted his action differently. Henry
S. Johnston had announced his candidacy for the senate, and a
Johnston versus Holloway campaign threatened to revive all of
the ill will associated with the impeachment. The Wentz
controversy also served as a barrier to the nomination.
Apparently, the suddenness of the announcement prevented
people from accepting it as truthful.[50]

Before Holloway's term of office ended, he encountered one
more political challenge. In November, 1930, two businessmen,
Robert E. Garnett of Oklahoma City and Earl R. Wilson of
Tulsa, filed a lawsuit against Holloway. They claimed he had
requested them to give R. L. Seaman, former secretary of the
highway department, a job in their business. Allegedly, the job
enabled Seaman to remain in Oklahoma City and testify at
Johnston's impeachment trial, and they wanted Holloway to
refund the wages they paid Seaman. The governor identified
Garnett and Wilson as part of a group attempting to embarrass
him because he refused to grant them favors. Holloway publicly
disclosed their requests and revealed: "Some demand the right

Officials and employees of the Oklahoma Historical Society and sponsoring legislators witness Acting Governor Holloway sign the bill authorizing a new building for the society (Oklahoma Publishing Company).

to dictate certain contracts with the highway department. Some urged special and unlawful favors to themselves in the state's public building program. Others requested the right to direct and control the adoption of textbooks and even at this moment are attempting the same thing."[51]

Shortly after denouncing these tactics, Holloway had the opportunity to perform a more pleasurable task. The Oklahoma Historical Society had started planning for the erection of a new building before Holloway had assumed office, and as acting governor, he had signed enabling and appropriation legislation for the new building on February 26, 1929. After becoming governor, he had informed the directors of the society that politics would not interfere in the building's construction and that he would only consult with them on details that required his attention. Holloway delivered a speech at the dedication of the completed building on November 15, 1930, and noted that

Governor William J. Holloway speaking at the dedication of Pioneer Woman statue in Ponca City, Oklahoma, on April 22, 1930 (William J. Holloway, Jr., Oklahoma City, Oklahoma).

its use and enjoyment by persons interested in Oklahoma's past would consecrate the state's history.[52]

Holloway's twenty-two months in the governor's office ended on January 12, 1931, but the conclusion of his tenure did not pass unrecognized. In a typical analysis of his administration, the *Tulsa World* noted that he had alleviated much of the political turmoil that had existed at the time of his inauguration. It attributed Holloway's success to his character and editorialized: "His personality and poise have been valuable and gratifying. The Holloway regime was conducted with responsibility and decorum."[53] Although the governor never sought a political office again, these same qualities served him well in private life.

Meanwhile, another Oklahoma governor put Holloway to work. Because of overproduction and regulatory problems in the petroleum industry, a number of oil producing states created the Interstate Oil Compact Commission. At the request of Governor Ernest W. Marland, a major instigator of the organization, Holloway served as one of Oklahoma's first representatives to the compact and was present at its creation on February 16, 1935. He continued to represent Oklahoma through the administrations of three governors, and in a 1944 meeting of the compact, he addressed its members and told them they should be sincere about the conservation of oil.[54] If they were not, he warned: "We must not . . . complain if the Federal government steps into the picture and sees to it that the petroleum reserves of America are properly protected and that oil and gas is produced along safe and sound conservation lines."[55]

Other organizations also benefited from Holloway's experience and commitment to public service. He maintained an active interest in political affairs and helped the Democratic Party win elections by working for its candidates, such as Robert S. Kerr on the state level and John F. Kennedy on the national level. His political advice and campaign endeavors earned him the position of elder statesman in the Democratic Party. When St. Luke's Methodist Church erected a new building, Holloway diligently raised funds for it. The construction of a fountain inside the church commemorating the career of Edgar S. Vaught, a federal judge, received his special attention.

Holloway always considered his gubernatorial service an honor that his party and the citizens of Oklahoma had bestowed upon him. This belief encouraged him to participate in public service work, but these activities also brought Holloway additional honors. The Oklahoma Heritage Association made him a member of the Oklahoma Hall of Fame in 1953. Many dignitaries and common people came to know him well and valued his friendship. In recognition of Holloway's service to Oklahoma, 800 of these friends gathered in Oklahoma City and gave him a surprise party for his seventy-sixth birthday.

At the end of Holloway's term of office in 1931, he stayed with his family in Oklahoma City and established a home. He started a successful law practice and remained in the legal profession for the rest of his life. His son, William J. Holloway, Jr., also entered the legal profession. When President Lyndon B. Johnson appointed his son to the United States Court of Appeals for the Tenth Circuit in 1968, the elder Holloway considered the appointment to be one of the major highlights of his life. Holloway suffered a heart attack in April, 1969, but he recovered and returned to work. Amy Holloway died on September 8, 1969, and he died, at the age of eighty-one, on January 28, 1970. He was buried in Rose Hill Cemetery in Oklahoma City.[56]

The honors conferred upon Holloway after service as governor reflected the high regard people had for him and demonstrated the effectiveness of a personal character that earned the respect of others. This trait played an important role in his governorship, and the political observers of his administration recognized it. Before he assumed office, a high degree of responsibility and decorum had not been dominant in Oklahoma politics, but he gave the state an image of commendable political ethics that it sorely needed.

Like most Oklahoma governors, Holloway experienced both failure and success in office. The legislature resisted the highway bond issue and tax reform. The citizens rejected organizational reform in higher education. Future economic conditions, caused by the Great Depression, would have made it difficult to retire the highway bonds, however. It was also doubtful if a climate of opinion existed that would have nurtured these reforms. Improved textbook adoption methods, centralized teacher certification, increased salaries for public officials, and reorganization of the highway commission became laws that the state needed. Although some of his appointments created controversy, his search for qualified officials benefited the state.

Governor Holloway presided over a transition period between the booming and boisterous twenties and the depression dominated thirties. Insinuations and charges against his administration were a residue of earlier practices. Attempts to ease the impact of economic depression were an indication of future governmental methods. With political skills developed in one decade, Holloway tried, ably and with some success, to guide Oklahoma into the next decade. Unfortunately for the state, he never sought another political office.

ENDNOTES

1 *Daily Oklahoman* (Oklahoma City), March 21, 1929, p. 13.

2 *Ibid.*, p. 1.

3 Joseph B. Thoburn and Muriel H. Wright, *Oklahoma: A History of the State and Its People*, 4 vols. (New York: Lewis Historical Publishing Company, 1929), Vol. III, p. 1; Gaston Litton, *History of Oklahoma at the Golden Anniversary of Statehood*, 4 vols. (New York: Lewis Historical Publishing Company, 1957), Vol. III, pp. 258-259; *Tulsa Tribune* (Tulsa), January 29, 1970, p. 1C; William J. Holloway, Jr., Interview, Oklahoma City, Oklahoma, October 3, 1977; *Daily Oklahoman*, March 21, 1929, p. 13.

4 *Daily Oklahoman*, March 21, 1929, p. 13; Thoburn and Wright, *Oklahoma: A History of the State and Its People*, Vol. III, p. l; Oklahoma Senate, *Journal of the Senate, Eighth Legislature, Regular Session, 1921* (Oklahoma City: Harlow Publishing Company, 1921), pp. 2000-2003.

5 Oklahoma Senate, *Journal of the Senate, 1921*, p. 2002.

6 Oklahoma Senate, *Journal of the Senate, Tenth Legislature, Regular Session, 1925* (Oklahoma City: Leader Press, 1925), pp. 1-7.

7 William J. Holloway, Jr., Interview; *Harlow's Weekly*, Vol. XXVII, No. 22 (November 28, 1925), p. 15.

8 *Harlow's Weekly*, Vol. XXVII, No. 22, p. 15; William J. Holloway to Henry G. Bennett, February 4, 1925, R. L. Evans to William H. Holloway, March 12, 1925, William J. Holloway Governor Papers, Oklahoma Archives and Records Division, Oklahoma Department of Libraries, Oklahoma City, Oklahoma. This collection of Holloway's papers contains a minimal amount of material. If other items are extant, they are not known.

9 Oklahoma Election Board, *Directory of the State of Oklahoma, 1931* (Oklahoma City: Oklahoma State Election Board, 1931), pp. 95-97; William J. Holloway, Jr., to Author, February 3, 1978; *Tulsa Tribune*, November 2, 1926, p. 1; *Harlow's Weekly*, Vol. XXIX, No. 30 (November 6, 1926), pp. 3-4.

10 Litton, *History of Oklahoma at the Golden Anniversary of Statehood*, Vol. I, pp. 566-568; *Harlow's Weekly*, Vol. XXIV, No. 9 (March 1, 1929), pp.4-6.

11 *Stillwater Gazette* (Stillwater), June 8, 1928, p. 1; *Tulsa Tribune*, January 29, 1970, p. 6C; *Harlow's Weekly*, Vol. XXXII, No. 23 (June 9, 1928), p. 4; William J. Holloway, Jr., Interview.

[12] *Daily Oklahoman*, January 22, 1929, p. 1, March 21, 1929, p. 13; *Harlow's Weekly*, Vol. XXXIV, No. 13 (March 30, 1929), p. 3.

[13] "Oklahoma's Impeachment Complex," *Literary Digest*, Vol. C, No. 6 (February 9, 1929), p. 12.

[14] William J. Holloway Interview, Oklahoma Living Legends Library, Oklahoma Christian College, Oklahoma City, Oklahoma.

[15] *Daily Oklahoman*, April 2, 1929, p. 1.

[16] Bryan Mack, "Oklahoma—Forty Years Young," *Review of Reviews*, Vol. LXXX, No. 3 (September, 1929), p. 134.

[17] *Daily Oklahoman*, March 22, 1929, pp. 1, 9.

[18] William J. Holloway Interview.

[19] Oklahoma House, *Journal of the House of Representatives, Twelfth Legislature, First Extraordinary Session, 1929*, 2 pts. (Oklahoma City: Leader Press, 1929), Pt. I, p. 44.

[20] *Harlow's Weekly*, Vol. XXXIV, No. 13 (March 30, 1929), p. 8, No. 17 (April 27, 1929), p. 7.

[21] *Daily Oklahoman*, July 6, 1929, p. 8.

[22] *Harlow's Weekly*, Vol. XXXIV, No. 13, p. 3; *Daily Oklahoman*, April 12, 1929, pp. 1-2.

[23] *Daily Oklahoman*, April 12, 1929, p. 1.

[24] Oklahoma Highway Commission, *Report of the State Highway Commission, 1929-1930* (Oklahoma City: Semco Color Press, 1930), pp. 12, 26, 36, 94.

[25] *Harlow's Weekly*, Vol. XXXIV, No. 13, p. 8, No. 18 (May 4, 1929), p. 3; Oklahoma House, *Journal of the House of Representatives, Twelfth Legislature, First Extraordinary Session, 1929*, Pt. I, pp. 23, 30.

[26] Oklahoma House, *Journal of the House of Representatives, Twelfth Legislature, First Extraordinary Session, 1929*, pp. 1-50.

[27] *Ibid.*, pp. 53, 836-845, Pt. II, pp. 1656, 2747; Oklahoma Highway Commission, *Report of the State Highway Commission, 1929-1930*, pp. 84-88.

[28] Oklahoma House, *Journal of the House of Representatives, Twelfth Legislature, First Extraordinary Session, 1929*, Pt. I, p. 28, Pt. II, pp. 1991-2008; *Harlow's Weekly*, Vol. XXXIV, No. 25 (June 22, 1929), p. 12, Vol. XXV, No. 1 (July 6, 1929), pp. 10-12.

[29] Oklahoma House, *Journal of the House of Representatives, Twelfth Legislature, First Extraordinary Session, 1929*, Pt. II, pp. 1816-1817.

[30] *Ibid.*, p. 2008; *Harlow's Weekly*, Vol. XXXV, No. 1, pp. 10-12.

[31] Oklahoma House, *Journal of the House of Representatives, Twelfth Legislature, First Extraordinary Session, 1929*, Pt. I, pp. 31, 34.

[32] *Ibid.*, pp. 31-36, 720, 744, Pt. II, pp. 1507, 2501; "Legislature Backs Separate Board Plan," *The A. and M. College Magazine*, Vol. II, No. 1 (September, 1930), p. 6; Schiller Scroggs and Henry G. Bennett, *The Beginnings of Coordination in Oklahoma* (Oklahoma City: Oklahoma State Coordinating Board for Higher Education, 1934), p. 5; *Tulsa Tribune*, November 7, 1930, p. 2.

[33] Oklahoma House, *Journal of the House of Representatives, Twelfth Legislature, First Extraordinary Session, 1929*, Pt. I, p. 37.

[34] *Ibid.*, p. 39, Pt. II, p. 2343; *Daily Oklahoman*, May 21, 1929, p. 1.

[35] Oklahoma House, *Journal of the House of Representatives, Twelfth Legislature, First Extraordinary Session, 1929*, Pt. I, pp. 46-47; Oklahoma House, *Journal of the House of Representatives, Thirteenth Legislature, Regular Session, 1931*, 2 vols. (Oklahoma City: Leader Press, 1931), Vol. I, pp. 27, 46; *Tulsa Tribune*, January 19, 1930, p. 19K.

[36] *Daily Oklahoman*, July 6, 1929, p. 1.

[37] *Ibid.*, July 7, 1929, p. 12A, July 6, 1929, p. 8.

[38] *Ibid.*, July 6, 1929, p. 8.

[39] *Ibid.*, May 28, 1929, p. 1, January 8, 1930, p. 1, January 14, 1930, p. 1; Interstate Oil Compact Commission, *A Summary of the Background, Organization, Purposes, and Functions of the Interstate Compact to Conserve Oil and Gas* (Oklahoma City: Interstate Oil Compact Commission, 1947), p. 1.

[40] Oklahoma Highway Commission, *Report of the Highway Commission, 1929-1930*, pp. 8, 11-12; Oklahoma House, *Journal of the House of Representatives, Thirteenth Legislature, Regular Session, 1931*, Vol. I, pp. 23-50.

[41] Oklahoma House, *Journal of the House of Representatives, Thirteenth Legislature, Regular Session, 1931*, Vol. I, pp. 23-50; Oklahoma Survey Commission, *Financing Oklahoma Schools* (Oklahoma City: Oklahoma Department of Education, 1930), pp. 1-3.

[42] *Daily Oklahoman*, December 15, 1968, p. 23A.

[43] Minutes of the Meeting of the Oklahoma Highway Commission, January 3, 1930, Oklahoma Archives and Records Division, Oklahoma Department of Libraries, Oklahoma City, Oklahoma.

[44] *Daily Oklahoman*, January 11, 1930, p. 1; *Tulsa World* (Tulsa), January 11, 1930, pp. 1,5; *Harlow's Weekly*, Vol. XXXVI, No. 3 (January 18, 1930), pp. 9-10.

[45] *Harlow's Weekly*, Vol. XXXVI, No. 3, p. 9.

[46] *Ponca City News* (Ponca City), January 13, 1930, p. 1.

[47] *Harlow's Weekly*, Vol. XXXVI, No. 4 (January 25, 1930), p. 4.

[48] Oklahoma House, *Journal of the House of Representatives, Twelfth Legislature, First Extraordinary Session, 1929*, Pt. I, p. 43.

[49] *Oklahoma City Times* (Oklahoma City), August 19, 1969, p. 12.

[50] *Daily Oklahoman*, January 20, 1930, p. 1; *Harlow's Weekly*, Vol. XXXVI, No. 4, p. 4.

[51] *Daily Oklahoman*, November 8, 1930, p. 1.

[52] Thomas H. Doyle, "History of the Oklahoma Historical Society," *The Chronicles of Oklahoma*, Vol. X, No. 2 (June, 1932), pp. 165-166; *Daily Oklahoman*, April 8, 1929, p. 1, November 16, 1930, p. 1.

[53] *Tulsa World*, January 8, 1931, p. 6.

[54] Interstate Oil Compact Commission, *A Summary of the Background, Organization, Purposes, and Functions of the Interstate Compact to Conserve Oil and Gas*, pp. 1-4; William J. Holloway, "Welcome Address," *Interstate Oil Compact Quarterly Bulletin*, Vol. III, No. 3 (October, 1944), pp. 6-8.

[55] Holloway, "Welcome Address," p. 8.

[56] William J. Holloway, Jr., Interview; William J. Holloway Records, Oklahoma Hall of Fame, Oklahoma Heritage Association, Oklahoma City, Oklahoma; *Daily Oklahoman*, January 29, 1969, pp. 1-2.

William Henry Murray

Governor of Oklahoma, 1931-1935

By Edda L. Bilger

William Henry Murray

On January 12, 1931, a crowd of more than 12,000 Oklahomans watched intently the inaugural ceremony of the new governor, William Henry Murray. Among them were many poor and unemployed, whose faces lit up when he pledged his dedication to their cause: "I realize the hardship of the farmer without seeds to plant, the starving children of the laboring man. I realize that thousands are tramping the roads, but by the Eternal God as long as I can utter a breath, they shall be taken care of."[1] Murray's concern for the underprivileged and his sincere intention of improving life for the masses had been the main reasons for his unprecedented victory in the race for governor in which he defeated the Republican contender, Ira A. Hill, by a majority of more that 93,000 votes.[2]

The people's trust was well-founded. Elected governor at the age of sixty-one, Murray had proven his honesty and devotion to the welfare of the populace in a public career that was already legendary in Oklahoma. He was born on November 21, 1869, near what is today Collinsville, Texas, the son of Uriah Dow Thomas Murray, and his wife, Elizabeth. His mother died in childbirth when he was fifteen months old, and her parents took care of the children until Uriah married Mary Jane Green in 1873. Young Murray and his two brothers lived from then on with their parents in Montague County, Texas, where his father was engaged in various enterprises and ultimately owned a wagon yard and feed barn for travelers. He also operated a butcher shop and grocery store in the village of Montague.

The three boys never became close to their stepmother, and in 1881 they ran away from home. Then only twelve years of age, Murray already had experience in driving and roping cattle and was accustomed to hard physical labor. His schooling had been poor and sporadic; he attended classes for a few weeks only, but his father taught him the rudiments of arithmetic and at Sunday School he had learned the alphabet. The boy, however, had a sharp mind and demonstrated a keen interest in nature, spending much time observing and studying animals. He also had a burning desire to learn, and set for himself the goal of getting a good education. Working at odd jobs, such as picking cotton, chopping wood, laboring as a tenant farmer, and selling books, he finally graduated from College Hill Institute in Springtown, Texas, in 1889, with a first grade teaching certificate. He always remembered his teacher, D. P. Hurley, with deep gratitude.

Murray began his career as a school teacher in rural Texas, but even before his graduation he had become interested in politics. In 1890, when a young teacher, he was elected a delegate to the Texas State Democratic Convention in San Antonio. At age twenty-three he ran for state senator and was defeated, but not discouraged. The aspiring young politician had early realized that he needed a thorough knowledge of the law. He studied law in his leisure time and continued to do so after he quit teaching in 1894, when he entered the newspaper business with his brother George in Corsicana, Texas. Judge John Rice tutored him privately in law, and Murray was admitted to the Texas Bar in 1897. He opened his first law practice in Fort Worth, but found it unremunerative. Quite abruptly he decided to leave for Indian Territory and settled in Tishomingo, then the capital of the Chickasaw Nation.[3]

As a lawyer in Tishomingo, Murray became deeply interested in the Indian way of life. Over the years he acquired a collection of more than 1,000 volumes on Indian culture. Noticing the corruption and criminality among many of the white settlers, he concluded that a man of integrity would "shine like a silver dollar." He explained: "I deliberately then decided to be a better man than perhaps I had otherwise been, by determining I would always be candid with the people, never deceiving them, never committing a fraud, keeping my promises and obligations."[4] His honesty won him the confidence of the Indians, and his law practice thrived. Soon, his knowledge of constitutional law brought him again into contact with politics, for Governor Douglas H. Johnston of the Chickasaw Nation appointed him to draft the bills of the Chickasaw Legislature.

In 1899, Murray became a citizen of the Chickasaw Nation when he married Governor Johnston's niece, Mary Alice Hearrell, a one-sixteenth Chickasaw Indian. His bride was a former student and then a teacher at nearby Bloomfield Academy for girls. As a citizen of the Chickasaw Nation, Murray was entitled to an allotment of land valued at about $5,000. He acquired a farm in what is now Johnston County and moved there with his young family in 1902 with the intention of devoting much of his time to studying constitutional government.

His expertise served him well when he represented the Chickasaw Nation as a delegate to the Sequoyah Constitutional Convention at Muskogee in 1905, and he was chosen as one of the authors of the proposed constitution. After the failure of the double statehood movement, Murray served as president of the Oklahoma Constitutional Convention in 1906, and became famous as the "Father of the Constitution." He was elected as a representative to the first Oklahoma Legislature and was the speaker of the house of representatives in 1907 and 1908. In 1910, he ran for governor, but was defeated by Lee Cruce in the primary election.

Murray supported Woodrow Wilson, whom he appreciated as a scholar, when he ran for president of the United States in 1912. In the same year, a dream came true when he was elected to the United States House of Representatives. But four years later he was defeated for reelection because he emphasized the need for war preparedness and expressed the opinion that the United States would be unable to keep out of World War I. This antagonized many immigrants from Germany and Austria-Hungary in north-central Oklahoma. Again he lost when he ran for governor in 1918.[5]

Disappointed in politics and weary in body and soul, Murray turned his interest to South America. From 1919 to 1924, he traveled extensively, visiting most of the Latin-American countries. He was so fascinated by these "new frontiers" that he undertook a colonization project in Bolivia. It failed, partly because the colonists were unwiling to endure the rough life of pioneers and the isolation from civilization, and partly because a new Bolivian government revoked the colony's concessions. Murray at last gave up and returned with his family to Oklahoma in 1929 after losing all of his investments. Despite his absence of five years, he had not been forgotten. A large crowd greeted him on his arrival at Tishomingo, and almost at once his friends beleaguered him to run for governor. A reunion of the members of Oklahoma Constitutional Convention convinced the now sixty-year-old Murray that he could count on many vigorous supporters in the state.

On January 9, 1930, Murray announced his candidacy on the Democratic ticket. His campaign, supported by small contributions, was run on a tight budget. Throughout the first months of 1930, the major newspapers of the state almost ignored him. A small weekly, the *Blue Valley Farmer*, became his mouthpiece and effective ally. Murray supporters distributed it in various counties every week, concentrating in areas where he was campaigning.[6]

In speeches, Murray addressed especially the middle class, which he defined as "lying between the privilege seeking and idle rich and the hopeless, indolent, idle poor."[7] He advocated economy in government and a system of taxation according to which every citizen and every corporation had to pay strictly in proportion to wealth. To achieve this, he proposed the abolition of the state ad valorem tax and in its stead the establishment of a gross income tax. Thus, he hoped to lift the burden off the overtaxed farmers and small businessmen and to make corporations and the wealthy assume a larger share. To combat unemployment, he called for federal aid. Anticipating the New Deal by three years, he proposed $3 billion in federal appropriations for road construction camps which would provide work relief for the nation's unemployed.[8]

Murray's name had not lost its magic. By midsummer, 1930, the metropolitan papers admitted his growing following among the people and denounced him as a demagogue and a radical. Murray was careful not to succumb to special interests and even declined offers to speak to lodges or churches so that no group could claim him as its candidate.[9]

In the primary in July, 1930, Murray scored a surprisingly easy victory over his most formidable Democratic opponent, Frank M. Buttram, an oil millionaire from Oklahoma City. His majority of 94,872 votes over Buttram in the runoff primary on August 12, 1930, was even more spectacular. In the following months, his campaign gained strength steadily. He was especially successful in rural areas, and even Republican papers conceded that he had won the confidence of the farmers. *Harlow's Weekly* attributed his success to the fact that he was the first farmer to be a candidate of a major party as well as to his ability in relating to the common people. Murray had long been known as a brilliant orator and a magnetic speaker who could hold an audience captive for hours.[10]

He was not so successful in the cities, where he met with strong opposition. His carelessness in clothing and manners often caused offense. Also, his domineering personality and his naive self-assurance antagonized many among the well-educated. Progressive Oklahomans rejected his ideas in regard to higher education as reactionary. In spite of his own very limited contact with public education, he felt competent to give advice on the fields of study to be taught at colleges and universities and unabashedly denounced the teaching of sociology, for instance, as superfluous. His proposal to cut down appropriations for higher education also caused opposition and fear that Oklahoma would regress under his governorship. Big business interests, on the other hand, feared his tax proposals and the loss of privileges under a Murray administration.[11]

Murray's program, however, was geared to the needs of the populace. The economic boom was over in Oklahoma, and the drought of 1930 brought the Great Depression to the state. Many businesses had to close and unemployed men roamed the countryside, looking for work. For some years the lot of the rural population of Oklahoma had deteriorated. Drought years made farming in western Oklahoma precarious, and over-cultivation had led to serious soil erosion. Low prices for wheat and cotton brought many farmers to the brink of disaster and they barely managed to meet their mortgage payments. In addition, between 1920 and 1930, farm values in many eastern counties had declined more than a third, but the farmers still had to go on paying off their high mortgages. From 1930-1933, 10 percent of all Oklahoma farms were sold either because of foreclosures or because their owners had gone bankrupt. Many parents could not afford to buy textbooks and, therefore, kept their children out of school.[12]

Even the oil industry, long Oklahoma's pride, was facing formidable difficulties. The discovery of the East Texas Field in 1929 resulted in an overproduction of oil that not only forced the price down but also endangered the banks whose securities were based on the one dollar per barrel price. Oklahoma had a proration or production-limiting law but Texas did not enforce proration. Small producers and independent companies were in danger of going bankrupt.[13]

Moreover, the state of Oklahoma was in financial trouble. The state indebtedness had risen to $8 million. Because of the Great Depression, revenues declined, and yet the poor and unemployed called on the state for assistance. Murray's program offered a reasonable approach toward a healthier economy. His forceful personality and his proverbial honesty inspired hope and trust, and in the general election on November 4, 1930, the people of Oklahoma expressed their confidence in him with a record majority of almost 100,000 votes.[14]

Murray saw clearly that the Great Depression was more than just a temporary slump in the economy. With characteristic

The inaugural ceremony of Governor William H. Murray at the Oklahoma Capitol on January 12, 1931 (Oklahoma Publishing Company).

bluntness he warned: "The next five years beginning with January and following will be the hardest times ever experienced in the history of the United States."[15] His main goals, therefore, were to soften the effects of the Great Depression by easing the tax burden on lower income people, to enforce strict economy in the administration of the state, and to procure aid for the destitute and unemployed.

Already in June, 1930, Murray had asked an old friend, Melvin Cornish, to write a tax commission bill. Consulting regularly with Murray, Cornish and Judge J. L. Cooke prepared the bill introduced in the house of representatives on January 6, 1931. It was passed so quickly by the legislature that the new governor could proudly sign it within a week after his inauguration. The newly created Oklahoma Tax Commission was composed of three members, Melvin Cornish, the chairman, Walter D. Humphrey, who had been a member of the Oklahoma Constitutional Convention, and John T. Bailey, a Republican. Its task was not only to assess all property on a fair and equal basis, but also to centralize the collection of state taxes. New guidelines led to a realistic assessment of corporate property which resulted in higher revenues for the state. The primary goal of the commission however, was to lower the state ad valorem tax, which had become oppressively high. Murray's dream of wholly abolishing the state ad valorem tax became a reality on August 15, 1933, when the Tax Reduction Amendment to the Oklahoma Constitution was adopted, which not only abolished the state property tax but also wiped out the last remnants of township government in Oklahoma by terminating the township levy. Also, the maximum ad valorem tax limit for local purposes was reduced by almost a third.[16]

To make up for the loss of state funds from these measures, new sources of revenue were needed. Murray was in favor of a graduated income tax and a selected sales tax for luxuries, such as cigarettes and cosmetics. He was to have difficulties with these tax proposals for more than two years. When the legislature adopted a completely unsatisfactory income tax bill in 1931, Murray put his proposal to the people in an initiative election in December, 1931. But in spite of his Fire-Bells Campaign waged almost single-handedly to push his measures, he was defeated. He had met with a formidable array of opponents: the press, with rare exception, was against his proposals, as were the teachers, the oil interests, the building and loan associations, as well as banks and corporations. Big business in general fought the income tax bill, which put a larger part of the tax burden on big incomes. Yet the defeat was an extremely narrow one, for Murray had carried fifty-two of the seventy-seven counties on the tax bill. This encouraged him to resume his fight.

Finally, in the special session of 1933, a revamped tax bill was enacted. Much to Murray's dissatisfaction, the legislature adopted a 1 percent general sales tax instead of a sales tax on luxuries only. The governor always felt that food, inexpensive clothing, and medicine should be tax-exempt for the sake of the poor. Although the actual tax reform was accomplished only after a long, wearisome struggle, the establishment of the Oklahoma Tax Commission alone was an important achievement of the first year of Murray's administration.[17]

The same year brought several crises which the new governor tackled and overcame with forceful action and unorthodox methods. They brought him into the national limelight and spread his reputation as the "fiery governor" from coast to coast. The oil crisis of 1931 developed because the production of oil vastly surpassed its consumption. By the fall of 1930, about ten million barrels of oil could be produced per day in the United States, yet the actual demand was for less than three million barrels a day. Proration was an obvious answer, but, as one producer stated: "All the oil men want proration but some only want control of the output for the other fellow."[18] Proration was not sufficiently enforced, and while the price for crude oil had been one dollar per barrel in January, 1931, it had dwindled to eighteen cents per barrel in July of the same year. Consequently, the state's revenues, which depended largely on the gross production tax for oil, declined. Besides that, the small, independent operators and the owners of stripper wells were at the edge of ruin.

On August 4, 1931, Governor Murray ordered the closing of 3,108 prorated oil wells and called out the Oklahoma National Guard to enforce his order.[19] The governor based his decision to close the wells on a statute of 1921, which prohibited oil production when the price sank beneath the actual value of crude oil. The effect of the shutdown was spectacular. After sixty-five days, the price per barrel had risen to eighty-five cents, and Murray rescinded his order. In January, 1932, the price was again at one dollar per barrel. The governor noted proudly: "This act was wholly mine and was the *greatest indivdual act* I ever did in my life—the most far-reaching, and the effect and consequences . . . the greatest—far greater than the public, even many of the oil men realized." He complained that only the stripper well owners, whose wells were not closed, were grateful for what he had done: "I have never had any expression

from oil men in Oklahoma of appreciation."[20] But the independent oil operators of San Angelo, Texas, sent him a
telegram, congratulating him on his courage and his integrity.
Subsequently, some companies violated the proration law and
Murray closed the Oklahoma City Oil Field in March, 1933. One
month later, the legislature passed a new law imposing harsh
fines for violations and providing for strict enforcement.[21]

The use of the Oklahoma National Guard became one of the
trademarks of Murray's administration. During his four years
in office, he called out the national guard no less than thirty-
four times. In some instances, as in the case of the closing of the
oil wells, it was probably justified. But the governor did not
hesitate to call the troops on miscellaneous occasions, be it to
guarantee the sale of skimmed milk to the poor or to close an
Oklahoma City park to blacks. He enjoyed his authority and he
used it to the fullest; the summoning of the national guard
expressed this power. Murray, however, also may have used the
national guard for quite a different reason: it symbolized not
only power but also action and change. At a time when the
economic situation looked hopeless, when no one seemed to be
able to control poverty and unemployment, the governor and
the national guard proved that success was still possible and that
the state government was capable of representing and assisting
the common people.

One such case was the so-called Bridge War. The states of
Oklahoma and Texas had built free bridges across the Red River
at Denison, Gainesville, and Ryan. The toll bridge company at
Denison, which had a contract with the state of Texas,
complained and obtained injunctions from federal courts in
Texas and in Oklahoma against the opening of the free bridge.
Murray called out the Oklahoma National Guard and enforced
free traffic over the new bridge, arguing that the federal courts
had no jurisdiction and that Oklahoma had not given permission
to the company to sue it. The governor's action was acclaimed
by the press, and a photograph of Murray, conversing with the
soldiers at the free bridge, appeared in many newspapers
through the United States with the caption: "Horatio at the
Bridge." The flamboyant Oklahoma governor became a favorite

Governor William H. Murray conversing with troops of the Oklahoma National Guard during the Bridge War between Oklahoma and Texas in 1931. This photograph appeared in many newspapers throughout the United States (Oklahoma Publishing Company).

subject of newspapermen and was featured in a number of national magazines. He also attracted attention with his speech at Lincoln's Tomb in Springfield, Illinois, on the occasion of Lincoln's birthday, and when he spoke to a crowd of 20,000 at Soldier's Field in Chicago on Labor Day, 1931.[22]

Murray's courage, decisiveness, and oratorical gifts had made him a nationally-known figure, and his friends and admirers envisioned him as the next president of the United States. He had supporters in many states, and an Oklahoma magazine claimed in January, 1932, that forty newspapers carried a regular column of his witty political remarks, called "Murrayisms." His picture made the title page of *Time Magazine* on February 29, 1932, less than a week after he formally announced his candidacy. True to his pledge to devote his work

The Oklahoma delegation with Governor William H. Murray at the Democratic National Convention in Chicago in 1932 (Western History Collections, University of Oklahoma).

to the welfare of the common man, he closed his announcement with these words: "I take this step only out of consideration of a profound sense of duty to the great middle class and the little men, for no one else seems to care to champion their cause."[23]

His campaign led him to many states, from North Dakota and Minnesota to Alabama, Florida, and Mississippi. It became known as the Bread, Butter, Bacon, and Beans Campaign. His platform provided for unemployment relief and for old age insurance. It championed the cause of the farmer and small businessman by the extension of credit and by the establishment of protective tariff laws. It promoted foreign commerce, especially with Mexico and the Latin-American countries. On the international level, Murray called for a reduction of armaments and opposed loans to foreign countries for the building of battleships and the purchase of weapons and ammunition. In South Carolina, the Oklahoman demanded a strong government, and expressed the need for "bread, butter and beans in private life and more brains and backbone in public life."[24]

As the principal speaker before the national convention of the Anti-Saloon League, Murray shocked his audience by a speech he said was "too wet for the dry and too dry for the wet," and by declaring: "I would hate to have it said that I rode into the White House astride a beer keg."[25] Murray won the attention of the newspapers, but he did not have the strong organization or the funds necessary for a successful campaign. One newspaper appraised him as "a ripsnortin' sincere and fearless man, friend of the people because he is of the people, who ought to but probably won't be elected President."[26] At the Democratic National Convention of 1932 in Chicago, Murray received twenty-three votes on the first ballot. One was the vote of his brother, a delegate to the convention from North Dakota, and the other twenty-two were those of the Oklahoma delegation.[27]

Back at home again, Governor Murray continued his power struggle with the former chairman of the Oklahoma Highway Commission, Louis (Lew) Haynes Wentz, a Ponca City oilman and philanthropist. Wentz had been appointed during Governor William J. Holloway's administration under a law of 1929 providing for staggered terms for the three commissioners. Wentz, a Republican, had been appointed for a six-year term and refused to resign when Murray became governor because of the latter's attacks against him during the election campaign. Under the law of 1929, members of the commission could only be dismissed for impeachable offenses. A long and bitter fight ensued which ended in 1933 when upon Murray's recommendation, the legislature changed the structure of the commission and created a new four-member commission. Wentz thus was removed, but Murray could not savor his victory. Under the new law, the senate had to confirm the governor's appointees and this restricted his control over the commission. Murray's attacks on Wentz, moreover, aroused the indignation and resentment of many Oklahomans, for Wentz was popular and highly regarded throughout the state. His work as commissioner was generally praised, and his philanthropic efforts in behalf of Oklahoma's colleges and the Crippled Children's Hospital in Oklahoma City were well-known. Even newspapers who were friendly toward the governor criticized him sharply, noting that the commission law of 1929 had been enacted to "remove roads from politics as far as possible," and that Murray had not acted in the best interest of the people, but for selfish political reasons.[28]

The dominant factor during the Murray administration, however, was the Great Depression. Natural disasters, like the droughts of 1930 and 1934, and the big flood of the Washita River in 1934, added to the misery of Oklahoma's people. The governor did his best to fulfill his inaugural pledge that the poor would receive care. Oklahoma, therefore, became the first state to appropriate state relief funds. An amount of $300,000 was provided to pay for food, clothing, fuel, and shelter for the needy, and an equal amount gave free seed to farmers who could not afford to buy it. Futher relief money was obtained through a one cent per gallon gasoline tax. These funds were inadequate, however, and Murray pushed a bill levying an emergency tax for relief purposes on the salaries of all public employees. It did not pass the legislature and, in an impassioned speech, the governor chastized the stunned legislators: "With men and women under the very shadow of the capitol begging for clothing and food, you with big salaries in your fine hotels cannot understand the danger."[29]

The governor realized that local and state aid were insufficient to combat the Great Depression and, in his opinion, federal aid was needed. The legislature adopted a resolution, upon his urging, requesting Congress to "enact legislation giving aid to the people of Oklahoma." The legislature also proposed to Congress to release the wheat stored and held by the United States Farm Relief Board so that the hungry could be fed. Murray went even further and called a general relief conference at Memphis, Tennessee, in the summer of 1931. Invited were state governors and members of the United States Congress. A second conference was held in the fall of the same year, but Congress was slow in reacting to the urgent pleas for action, and it was only in the summer of 1932 that federal funds became available through the Emergency Relief and Construction Act.[30]

In the meantime, Murray made every effort to give aid speedily with as little red tape as possible. Throughout the year 1931, he advised farmers to plant more vegetables than normally. In the fall he sent trucks with unemployed laborers to the farms, where the workers helped with the harvest and were paid in kind. Before winter set in, the relief money appropriated by the state had run out, and Murray gave part of his own salary to continue aid to the poor; he also asked government employees to contribute to a special relief fund. During the winter of 1931-1932, volunteers in Oklahoma City begged for unsalable groceries and produce from markets and restaurants. Soup kitchens were set up, and according to Murray, ten thousand people were taken care of in this way. He also saw to it that St. Anthony's Hospital in Oklahoma City could continue to feed hungry people through its soupline, and that skimmed milk was sold inexpensively to the poor, even though in both cases the Oklahoma Health Department had interfered.[31]

Unemployed workers who went from town to town looking for work became a common sight during the Great Depression, and often they were arrested and jailed for vagrancy. Governor

Murray condemned these arrests as unjustified and on one occasion ordered the release of 163 such men. In his opinion, the vagrancy law was only intended for beggars who were unwilling to work. In order to provide shelter for migratory laborers in search of work, transient relief centers were established with federal funds in 1934. Murray also opposed sharply the practice of sending debtors to jail for failure of paying their debts and sought to prevent the foreclosure of mortagages on homes. He understood the despair and the helplessness of the people and sympathized with them when they openly began to resist foreclosure sales. In February, 1933, a crowd of 1,300 stopped such a sale at Cherokee, and farmers formed a "council of defense" to protect their homes.[32] In a special executive message to the legislature, Murray admonished the lawmakers to enact a bill which would give the home owners an extension of time. He warned that the incident at Cherokee was just a beginning and said: "You must keep in mind that these men are not anarchists; not communists; but American citizens with their 'backs to the wall,' fighting for the preservation of their homes and the security of their families."[33]

One year later, Governor Murray prevented the sale of houses and farms of owners unable to pay taxes and penalties by issuing executive orders remitting and commuting all penalties for taxes on real estate. When some county treasurers ignored these orders, he authorized the Oklahoma National Guard to prevent the sales by military force, because, as he explained: "The protection of the homes of the people in stressful times like these is a vital policy transcending any temporary loss of taxes."[34]

In the summer of 1932, additional federal relief funds became available as loans from the Reconstruction Finance Corporation. With this money, dams, lakes, and farm-to-market roads were constructed. Murray controlled these funds jealously and always saw to it that he kept reserves. He was able, therefore, to spend $267,000 on textbooks for the children of relief recipients. His dream that every child should receive free textbooks was realized many years later when the legislature passed a free textbook law in 1947. The fact he could spend such a large sum on textbooks caused much speculation and criticism. While his honesty was not questioned, his arbitrary and secret management of the funds brought resentment.[35]

The influx of federal relief money was to be a double-edged sword for Murray. It became a lifesaver for Oklahoma, but entailed endless difficulties and frustrations for the governor. In the spring of 1933, Congress established three agencies designed to give direct relief to the poor, to provide employment, and to carry out conservation and public works projects: the Federal Emergency Relief Administration, the Civilian Conservation Corps, and the National Industrial Recovery Administration. One-half billion dollars of relief money was allotted to the states through the Federal Emergency Relief Administration under Harry L. Hopkins. The state governors were responsible for the funds allocated to their state. Oklahoma received funds for direct relief or charity as well as for work relief. Parks were improved, schools built, and flood control work was done. The most ambitious project was the construction of Lake Murray, which employed between 900 and 1,500 men during a given week. Workers were rotated every week so that as many as possible could benefit from the federal funds.

Within a few months, however, rumors circulated that relief money in Oklahoma was fraudulently used, and charges of inexcusable waste and favoritism were raised. Senator Thomas P. Gore of Oklahoma introduced an amendment to the 1933-1934 federal aids bill providing that the funds could but did not have to be handled by the state governors. Some newspapers suspected political motives behind the move, since Murray was a potential opponent of Gore in the 1936 race for United States senator. Hopkins investigated the situation in Oklahoma; he exonerated Murray and concluded: "I've heard that too much was allowed for administration of relief in this state. My feeling is that probably too little is spent for that."[36]

Statistics of the Federal Emergency Relief Administration in Washington showed in December, 1933, that 27 percent of all families in Oklahoma received unemployment relief. By that time new charges had been made against Murray and tensions had developed between him and Hopkins which made further cooperation impossible.[37] In a letter to Oklahoma Congressman Tom D. McKeown, Murray stated: "the federal representatives persist in an effort to compel me to accept money, and then let them or other authority make the payroll, leaving the governor only to sign on the dotted line."[38] Murray demanded either full authority over the funds or relief from this responsibility. In February, 1934, Carl Giles was placed in charge of federal relief funds in Oklahoma, while Murray still handled state relief work dispensing cash and commodities. Beginning in March, 1934, federal funds, withheld for about two months because of difficulties between Murray and Hopkins, flowed again into Oklahoma at a rate of $2 million a month. This money was dispensed and audited by federal employees.[39]

The second agency of utmost importance to Oklahomans was the Civil Works Administration, which gave jobs to 100,000 men and women during the winter of 1933-1934. A survey at that time revealed that more than 300,000 persons were out of work in Oklahoma. Of great benefit also to Oklahoma was the Civilian Conservation Corps, which established sixty-four camps in Oklahoma, among them three in Oklahoma City and Tulsa, where the corps developed Oklahoma City's Lincoln Park and Tulsa's Mohawk Park. Thousands of young men were enrolled in these camps for a period of six months and were employed in reforestation and other conservation projects.[40]

During the summer of 1933, an extreme drought hit the Southwest. Governor Murray, who strongly believed in cooperation between states who shared problems, called a conference at Guymon, Oklahoma, of representatives of the states of Oklahoma, Colorado, Kansas, New Mexico, and Texas. The conference requested that the National Industrial Recovery Administration appropriate $98 million for relief in the drought region. Of this sum, $54 million should be spent to construct lakes throughout Oklahoma. A public works program had been authorized in June, 1933, to carry out projects "for the conservation and development of natural resources, including control, utilization and purification of water and the prevention of soil or coastal erosion."[41]

During the following months, Oklahoma had high hopes of securing a fair share of the $3.3 billion public works fund for the lakes project. Governor Murray created the Department of Waterways, Power, and Flood Control which became a part of the Oklahoma Conservation Commission in 1935. It consisted of three members, who were to work in close cooperation with the Secretary of the Interior. At first the interstate conference at Guymon seemed successful, and a board was appointed that came to be known as the Arkansas River Basin Commission, composed of representatives of the states of Oklahoma, Arkansas, Kansas, Missouri, New Mexico, Colorado, and Texas. But in February, 1934, the commission was abolished.[42]

The *Daily Oklahoman* charged that Oklahoma was the "step-child of the nation on public works," declaring that the state was only thirty-fourth in line and was to receive less than two-thirds of 1 percent of the allotments. Congressman Wesley E. Disney, who had introduced a complete flood control bill affecting the seven states, complained that the project had not been given a fair deal. The necessity of flood control was forcefully brought home, when the Hammon flood of the Washita River on April 6, 1934, claimed seventeen lives and caused many millions of dollars in damage. Both flood control and drought prevention appeared necessary.

Murray had started the construction of more than ninety ponds west of the Rock Island Railway. On some of the lakes, work was continued after he ceased to manage the federal funds, but many of the projects were abandoned. Only the devastating drought of 1934 renewed public interest in the lake building program.[43]

The first three years of Murray's administration were characterized by dramatic incidents, much publicity, and his relentless struggle to overcome the Great Depression. In spite of the governor's economy measures, the state's indebtedness had risen to $11.5 million. Oklahoma treasury bonds were issued to pay for state warrants and were retired by revenue from gasoline taxes. When Murray entered office, state warrants sold at a discount. He brought them up to par and kept them at par during his term. Oklahoma treasury bonds were even sold above par in New York, a sign that Oklahoma's financial standing was considered healthy. Not even Murray's enemies criticized his handling of the state's finances.[44]

The election of Murray's successsor became the major political issue of 1934. Ernest W. Marland, an oilman from Ponca City, and Tom Anglin, the speaker of the house of representatives, vied for the Democratic nomination. Marland promised "to bring the New Deal to Oklahoma," which was ironic since the state had been sustained by the New Deal for the past one-and-one-half years. The real issue was whether Murray would be able to control the election with his support of Anglin. Marland in the primary received a plurality of 55,000 votes more than Anglin, but Anglin withdrew from the runoff primary. The newspapers saw in the result not so much a vote against Anglin as a vote against Murray. The *Daily Oklahoman* noted somewhat regretfully: "Some of the best men that ever sought or held public office in Oklahoma have been hurled back into private life by voters who are determined to do their own voting and keep the franchise free."[45] Marland won the general election against the Republican candidate, William B. Pine, with a majority of 80,000 votes.[46]

After the inauguration of Marland, Murray and his wife and daughter left the capital to return to Tishomingo. For some months he traveled, visiting the places of his childhood and youth in Texas. He then bought a small farm at Broken Bow and made his home there until his wife died in 1938. But it was not his nature to retire, and the summer of 1937 found him already preparing to run again for governor. Since his retirement from office, he had become bitter about President Franklin D. Roosevelt and the New Deal, and attacked both in speeches and lectures. The president revenged himself during a speaking tour in Oklahoma in 1938 and denounced Murray as "nationally known as a Republican."[47] Murray himself attributed his defeat in the primary of 1938 to Roosevelt's speeches. He continued to be politically active, however, and campaigned in 1940 for Wendell L. Willkie, the Republican candidate for president. He openly opposed the entry of the United States into World War II. His views became more and more extreme, and in his later years he was known for his blatant anti-Semitic and anti-black attitude. He turned to writing and authored several books, the most important of them being his *Memoirs of Governor Murray and True History of Oklahoma*, in three volumes. This publication appeared in 1945 and contained many of his political speeches.

A highpoint in Murray's old age was the inauguration of his son, Johnston, as governor of Oklahoma, in 1951, twenty years to the month after his own inauguration in the same office. The former governor became blind and deaf in his last years. In 1956, he suffered a stroke of apoplexy and fell sick with pneumonia. He did not recover and died on October 15, 1956, in Oklahoma City, and was buried in the cemetery at Tishomingo at his wife's side.[48]

As governor, Murray was gifted with qualities and abilities which made him a noteworthy leader. He also possessed traits that hindered his effectiveness and were potentially dangerous to his constituents. As a specialist in constitutional law, he was an asset to the legislature and helped in writing important legislation such as the bill establishing the Oklahoma Tax Commission. His intimate knowledge of the United States Constitution, as well as of the Oklahoma Constitution, was the basis for his swift and far-reaching action in the closing of oil wells as well as in his timely action in the Bridge War.

Murray was conscientious and farsighted in his management of Oklahoma's natural and financial resources. He not only assessed present conditions, but envisioned future developments. When the state was virtually flooded with oil, he foresaw the day when it would be exhausted. He was concerned with the problems of soil erosion and of flood and drought control, and established the Department of Waterways, Power, and Flood Control as a step toward their solution.

Murray's concern and care reached out to those whose way of life was threatened by exploitation, depression, and drought. He knew that the problems caused by the Great Depression could be solved best in cooperation with those who were affected. His interstate conferences on oil proration, relief, drought, and flood control resulted from this viewpoint. He insisted that government should help the people help themselves and,

Governor William H. Murray during his Fire-Bells Campaign in 1931 for income tax reform (Oklahoma Publishing Company).

therefore, was much in favor of work relief which aided the unemployed as well as society.

Murray's establishment of the Oklahoma Tax Commission, the abolishment of the ad valorem tax for state purposes, and a more equal distribution of the tax burden through the new income and sales taxes helped especially the lower and middle income classes at the height of the Great Depression. These measures also helped to stablize the state's finances.

Murray's administration could have been more successful and his proposals could have been enacted earlier if his domineering personality had not aroused resistance and antagonism. He was too self-assured, he did not like advice, and he meddled in areas in which he was not competent, such as higher education. Consequently, he lost the goodwill and cooperation of many progressive Oklahomans. Although Murray was controversial, he served as governor of Oklahoma at the right time. His blunt honesty and his sincere concern for the welfare of all Oklahomans gave his constituents a sense of security. He did not betray their trust.

ENDNOTES

1 *Tulsa Tribune* (Tulsa), January 12, 1931, p.8.

2 Oklahoma House, *Journal of the House of Representatives, Thirteenth Legislature, Regular Session, 1931* (Oklahoma City: Leader Press, 1931), p. 8.

3 William H. Murray, *Memoirs of Governor Murray and True History of Oklahoma* (3 vols., Boston: Meador Publishing Company, 1945), Vol. I, pp. 43-199, throughout, Vol. III, p. 101.

4 *Ibid.*, Vol. I, p. 233.

5 *Ibid.*, pp. 233-315, Vol. II, pp. 7-62, 112-163, 213; Oklahoma Election Board, *Directory of Oklahoma, 1975* (Oklahoma City: Oklahoma Election Board, 1975), p. 431.

6 Murray, *Memoirs*, Vol. II, pp. 233-368.

7 *Ibid.*, Vol. III, p. 560.

8 *Ibid.*, pp. 560-569, Vol. II, p. 388; *Harlow's Weekly*, Vol. XXXVI, No. 16 (April 19, 1930), p. 11.

9 *Harlow's Weekly*, Vol. XXXVI, No. 28 (July 12, 1930), p. 4; *Oklahoma News* (Oklahoma City), July 2, 1930, p. 2 ; Murray, *Memoirs*, Vol. II, pp. 376-377.

10 *Daily Oklahoman* (Oklahoma City), August 13, 1930, p. 1; *Lawton News Review* (Lawton), October 9, 1930, p. 2 ; *Harlow's Weekly*, Vol. XXXVI, No. 41 (October 18, 1930), pp. 9-10.

11 Murray, *Memoirs*, Vol. III, p. 564; *Country Gentleman* (Philadelphia, Pennsylvania), Vol. CII, No. 1 (January, 1932), p. 4.

12 Judith Anne Gilbert, "Migrations of the Oklahoma Farm Population 1930 to 1940" (Unpublished Master of Arts Thesis, Norman: University of Oklahoma, 1965), pp. 41, 54.

13 *Harlow's Weekly*, Vol. XXXIX, No. 39 (September 24, 1932), p. 4; Murray, *Memoirs*, Vol. II, pp. 502-503.

14 Murray, *Memoirs*, Vol. II, p. 435.

15 *Daily Oklahoman*, January 1, 1931, p. 2.

16 Murray, *Memoirs*, Vol. II, pp. 394-395; Oklahoma Legislature, *Session Laws of 1931* (Oklahoma City: Harlow Publishing Company, 1931), pp. 219-223; *Harlow's Weekly*, Vol. XLI, No. 7 (August 19, 1933), p. 9; Oklahoma Legislature, *Session Laws of 1933* (Guthrie: Co-operative Publishing Company, 1933), pp. 386-387; Oklahoma Legislature, *Oklahoma Statutes, 1931: Supplement, 1936* (Oklahoma City: Harlow Publishing Corpration, 1936), p. 1181.

17 *Harlow's Weekly*, Vol. XXXVII, No. 6 (February 7, 1931), p. 5, Vol. XXXVIII, No. 26 (December 26, 1931), p. 7; Oklahoma Legislature, *Session Laws of 1933*, pp. 456-465, 426.

18 *Harlow's Weekly*, Vol. XXXIX, No. 39 (September 24, 1932), p. 4.

19 *Daily Oklahoman*, August 5, 1931, p. 1.

20 Murray, *Memoirs*, Vol. II, p. 510.

21 *Blue Valley Farmer* (Oklahoma City), August 6, 1931, p. 1; Oklahoma Legislature, *Session Laws of 1933*, pp. 278-301.

22 *Daily Oklahoman*, July 17, 1931, p. 1, February 12, 1931, p. 1, Murray, *Memoirs*, Vol. II, pp. 496-501; *Daily Oklahoman*, September 8,1931, p. 1.

23 *Harlow's Weekly*, Vol. XXXIX, No. 3 (January 16, 1932), p. 13; *Time Magazine*, Vol. XIX, No. 9 (February 29, 1932), p. 14; *Harlow's Weekly*, Vol. XXXIX, No. 9 (February 29, 1932), p. 14; *Harlow's Weekly*, Vol. XXXIX, No. 9 (February 27, 1932), p. 13, 14.

24 Gordon Hines, *Alfalfa Bill: An Intimate Biography* (Oklahoma City: Oklahoma Press, 1932),pp. 306-307; *Harlow's Weekly*, Vol. XXXIX, No. 5 (January 30, 1932), p. 13.

25 *New York Times* (New York, New York), January 19, 1932, p. 17.

26 *Harlow's Weekly*, Vol. XXXIX, No. 5 (January 30, 1932), p. 13.

27 Keith Bryant, *Alfalfa Bill Murray* (Norman: University of Oklahoma Press, 1968), p. 236.

28 *Harlow's Weekly*, Vol. XXXIX, No. 15 (April 9. 1932), p. 12.

29 Oklahoma Legislature, *Session Laws of.1931*, pp. 351, 354; *Daily Oklahoman*, February 5, 1931, p. 1.

30 *Harlow's Weekly*, Vol. XXXVIII, No. 9 (August 29, 1931), p. 5.

31 Murray, *Memoirs*, Vol. II, pp. 458-460, 527-528; Norman W. Cooper, "Oklahoma in the Great Depression, 1930-1940: The Problem of Emergency Relief (Unpublished Master's of Arts Thesis, Norman: University of Oklahoma, 1973), pp. 25-28.

32 Murray, *Memoirs*, Vol. II, pp. 568-569; *Harlow's Weekly*, Vol. XLII, No. 10 (March 17, 1934), p. 13, Vol. XL, No. 5 (February 4, 1933), p. 4.

33 Oklahoma House, *Journal of the House of Representatives, Fourteenth Legislature, Regular Session, 1933* (Oklahoma City: Leader Press, 1933), pp. 765-767.

34 Oklahoma, Files of the Secretary of State, Executive Order Nos. 1709-1714, April 9, 11, 12, 14, 1934, Archives and Records Division, Oklahoma Department of Libraries, Oklahoma City, Oklahoma.

35 Cooper, "Oklahoma in the Great Depression, 1930-1940: The Problem of Emergency Relief," throughout; Murray, *Memoirs*, Vol. II, p. 533; Oklahoma Legislature, *Official Session Laws of 1947* (Guthrie: Co-operative Publishing Company, 1947), p. 531.

36 William E. Leuchtenburg, *Franklin D. Roosevelt and the New Deal* (New York: Harper and Row, 1963), p. 120; *Harlow's Weekly*, Vol. XL, No. 5 (February 4, 1933), p. 4, Vol. XLI, No. 2 (July 8, 1933), p. 8, Vol. XLI, No. 8 (August 26, 1933), p. 6

37 *Harlow's Weekly*, Vol. XLI, No. 26 (December 30, 1933), p. 11.

38 *Ibid.*, Vol. XLII, No. 2 (January 13, 1934), p. 13.

39 *Ibid.*, Vol. XLII, No. 8 (February 24,1934), p. 9.

40 *Ibid.*, Vol. XLI, No. 23 (December 9, 1933), p. 10, Vol. XLII, No. 1 (January 6, 1934), p. 11, Vol. XLII, No. 13 (April 7, 1934), p. 12; Reid Holland, "The Civilian Conservation Corps in the City: Tulsa and Oklahoma City in the 1930's," *The Chronicles of Oklahoma*, Vol. LIII, No. 3 (Fall, 1975), pp. 368-369.

41 *Harlow's Weekly*, Vol. XLI, No. 4 (July 22, 1933), p. 14; Bess Farley Duckworth, "History of Soil Conservation in Oklahoma" (Unpublished Master of Education Thesis, Norman: University of Oklahoma, 1940), pp. 12, 13.

42 *Harlow's Weekly*, Vol. XLII, No. 2 (January 13, 1934), p. 11, Vol. XLI, No. 8 (August 26,

1933), p. 4, Vol. XLI, No. 10 (September 9, 1933), p. 5, Vol. XLII, No. 8 (February 24, 1934), p. 15, Vol. XLII, No. 14 (April 14, 1934), p. 12.

[43] *Daily Oklahoman*, February 27, 1934, p. 2; United States Department of Agriculture, *The Washita* (Stillwater: Soil Conservation Service, 1964), throughout.

[44] Murray, *Memoirs*, Vol. II, p. 435; *Harlow's Weekly*, Vol. XLIII, No. 20 (December 1, 1934), p. 14.

[45] *Daily Oklahoman*, July 26, 1934, p. 8; Bryant, *Alfalfa Bill Murray*, p. 252.

[46] Oklahoma House, *Journal of the House of Representatives, Seventeenth Legislature, Regular Session* (Oklahoma City: Leader Press, 1939), p. 22 ; Oklahoma Election Board, *Directory of Oklahoma, 1975*, p. 467.

[47] Murray, *Memoirs*, Vol. III, pp. 7, 11; Bryant, *Alfalfa Bill Murray*, p. 263.

[48] Murray, *Memoirs*, Vol. III, pp. 14-16, 28; *Daily Oklahoman*, October 16, 1956, p. 1.

Ernest Whitworth Marland

Governor of Oklahoma, 1935-1939

By Michael W. Everman

Ernest Whitworth Marland

"Mr. Chairman, this is probably the last occasion upon which I, as a member, will address you and this House." Ernest Whitworth Marland, a freshman congressman from Oklahoma's Eighth District, went on to explain in April, 1934, that he was leaving his seat in the United States House of Representatives to seek the office of governor "because the financial and economic situation of my state is so grave and requires the type of business leadership I feel that I can supply." He pointed out the paradoxical situation in which Oklahomans had "produced billions in wealth and still do produce fabulously, but we are facing bankruptcy." He attributed this situation to "bad government, lack of business management of state affairs, and entire failure of economic planning." To demonstrate his point, he offered the fact that "Oklahoma produced last year enough food for 10 times her own population but could not feed her own." In closing, he stated: "We cannot abide famine in our land of abundance. If the people of Oklahoma will have me as their Governor I expect to give the rest of my public life in their service." Marland was foregoing almost certain reelection to

Congress in his effort to bring Oklahoma out of the Great Depression.[1]

Marland was born in Pittsburgh, Pennsylvania, on May 8, 1874, the son of Alfred and Sara Marland. His father was a relatively prosperous ironmaster. Ernest received his early education at a boarding school in eastern Tennesee, but finished high school in Pittsburgh. He received a law degree from the University of Michigan at the age of nineteen. By twenty-one, he had been admitted to the state bar of Pennsylvania and was practicing law on his own.[2]

One of Marland's major occupations as a lawyer was checking land titles and drawing up contracts in the coal and oil fields of Pennsylvania and West Virginia. This activity led him to become involved in the process of discovering coal and oil on his own. He studied geology and engineering and applied the knowledge he gained to his efforts to discover and market coal and oil. These attempts were handsomely rewarded when he struck oil and gas in West Virginia. By development of his new enterprise, he accumulated a small fortune. His prosperity was short-lived, however, for he lost his holdings in the banking panic in 1907, and found himself once again on his own.[3]

Following this stroke of misfortune, Marland decided to journey to the young state of Oklahoma to try his hand at the many possibilities for the development of its untapped resources. Arriving in December, 1908, he visited the Miller Brothers 101 Ranch near Ponca City. While on the ranch, Marland took advantage of the opportunity to tour the surrounding area. His background in the study of geological formations prompted him to speculate that underneath the rolling prairie lands of northern Oklahoma lay vast quantities of oil and gas. Consequently, he obtained leases to drill on several likely tracts of land, some owned by the Ponca Indians. He placed his money and hopes for success on the drilling of a wildcat well. His theory was proven when the well produced gas. Taking heart from this initial success and the many which followed, Marland and several associates formed the 101 Ranch Oil Company and the Kay County Gas Company. The expansion of drilling and the further discovery of oil and gas led to the establishment of the

Marland Refining Company of Oklahoma, which included in its operation such aspects as the building of pipelines, refineries, offices, and tank farms. By 1921, all of Marland's operations were combined under the umbrella of the Marland Oil Company, and he stood at the helm of a vast oil empire throughout most of the 1920s.[4]

Marland attained great stature in the Ponca City area as well as in the state and nation. His status in the community was reflected in his lifestyle. He first resided in an elaborate townhouse, but later lived in a more commodious mansion surrounded by beautiful formal gardens. In this location he sponsored frequent social activities, including such unusual touches as fox hunts and polo parties. As a prominent citizen and the employer of thousands of people, he contributed greatly to the growth and development of Ponca City. He gave readily and generously to charities and civic enterprises, built and maintained a golf course open to the public, and aided in the construction and support of parks, a hospital, and a children's home. He gave freely of his time and money to allow some of his good fortune and wealth to trickle down to his fellow men and improve their lives. He constructed homes for his employees and provided numerous additional benefits of inestimable service to them and gained for him their affection and loyalty. Perhaps his best-known contribution is the statue of the Pioneer Woman in Ponca City, which he sponsored at considerable personal expense to commemorate the heroic spirit of frontier women who contributed so much to the development of Oklahoma and the West.

Marland lived on his large Ponca City estate with his wife, Mary, and adopted son and daughter, George and Lyde. Mary died in 1926, and Marland married his ward Lyde in 1928. Lyde was to become the first lady of Oklahoma when Marland became governor.[5]

Marland's oil empire continued to prosper and expand throughout the 1920s. In order to meet the expenses required by expansion, Marland had to borrow extensively from several banks in the Southwest. In 1923, Marland, following the advice of banking wizard J. Pierpont Morgan, Jr., consolidated his

The Pioneer Woman statue in Ponca City sponsored by Marland before he became governor to commemorate the heroic spirit of the frontier women who helped develop the United States (Oklahoma Historical Society).

financial obligations into one bank, the Guaranty Trust Company of New York. As this relationship developed, the bankers, in return for their financial offerings, demanded and received a voice in the direction of company policy. By persistently vetoing Marland's proposals for the development of the company and by replacing Marland men with men of their own choosing, the bankers effectively wrenched control of Marland's company from his hands. Having been phased out of his own operation and relegated to a figurehead position, Marland resigned as president and chairman of the board of the Marland Oil Company in October, 1928. Shortly thereafter, the company merged with the Continental Oil Company. The name Marland was painted out of the familar red triangle symbol and replaced by Conoco. This experience with the large money interests and the subsequent loss of his fortune was a bitter experience for Marland.[6]

In 1932, Marland ran for the office of United States congressman from the Eighth District. He defeated the incumbent, Republican Milton C. Garber of Enid, and became the first Democrat to serve in that office. Marland's past experience was reflected in his actions in the nation's capital. While in Congress, Marland consistently fought the big money interests by endorsing legislation which would restrict the activities of banking interests and dilute their power over the nation's economy, with which he was painfully familiar. He was particularly interested in insuring the conservation and wise use of the nation's valuable oil resources and the equality of opportunity for small and independent producers in competition with the large conglomerates. He advocated the subsistence homestead, such as he had provided for many of his employees, as one solution to the economic woes of modest income people, particularly in Oklahoma. Marland, like most of his colleagues in Congress, supported the New Deal policies of President Franklin D. Roosevelt. These policies, with the hope of millions of Americans resting on their success, caught Marland's attention and seemed to call for the assistance of sympathetic leaders on the state level.[7]

In 1934, Marland sought to gain the nomination of the Democratic Party for governor. He based his campaign on the promise of bringing the New Deal to Oklahoma. His campaign was carried on by his followers until he had completed his duties in Congress, but upon his return to the state an intensive primary battle took place. The bandwagon appeal of the New Deal compaign garnered the highest number of votes in the primary election for Marland. In second place was Tom Anglin, the speaker of the Oklahoma House of Representatives, who carried the endorsement of the incumbent governor, William H. Murray. The need for a runoff primary was removed when Anglin, in a move applauded by the state press, withdrew from the race. Anglin justified his action by stating that in view of the more than 50,000 vote margin held by Marland in the primary, it would be better for the state and the party if he stepped aside and let Marland have the nomination of the Democratic Party.[8]

Oklahomans were apparently ready for the coming of the New Deal, for in the November, 1934, general election Marland defeated the Republican candidate, former United States Senator William B. Pine, by a margin of more than 120,000 votes. Marland immediately set to work making plans for implementing his program. He appointed several voluntary committees to aid him in the study of various problems confronting the state. He began by informing the public about his plans and conferred frequently with newly-elected legislators about prospects for his administraton.[9]

Marland had promised throughout his campaign to support and work with the national recovery program of President Roosevelt and to solve the pressing problem of unemployment in the state. He planned as governor to put into effect a businesslike administration of government and to utilize economic planning in carrying out his program. His background as a former industrialist and his experience while a congressman in Washington, D. C., equipped him to bring the New Deal to Oklahoma. The Great Depression had demonstrated that the old order of governmental and economic activity had not kept pace with rapid change in the United States. In order to repair the damage done by the depression, new policies would need to be introduced and accepted. The severe and unusual situation called for what seemed to many people to be drastic and different solutions. The new idea of the role of government as a tool to insure the well-being of the governed was what Marland wanted to place in effect in Oklahoma.[10]

In order to facilitate the implementation of his program, Marland needed to achieve some sort of a working relationship with the Oklahoma Legislature—the body which would place it in effect and could therefore spell the success or failure of his administration. The Democrats, who controlled both houses, had selected the leaders for the upcoming 1935 leglislative session. Selected to the powerful position of speaker of the house of representatives was Leon C. "Red" Phillips of Okemah. Claud Briggs of Wilburton was chosen president pro tempore of the senate. On January 5, 1935, shortly before taking office, governor-elect Marland conferred with Briggs, Phillips, and several other legislators at his home in Ponca City and outlined his proposals. He stressed the need for emergency relief appropriations for those unable to work and for elderly persons, and asked that both be given priority in the approaching legislative session. He indicated to these legislative leaders his basic proposals and asked for their support and cooperation in carring his program through.[11]

Marland took the oath of office as governor on January 14, 1935, following a somewhat tense but polite session with the outgoing governor, William H. Murray, who disagreed with him politically. In his inaugural address, he emphasized the need for the reconstruction of governmental and economic theories to meet the prevailing situation. He urged cooperation with the Roosevelt program for recovery and forewarned the people of Oklahoma that new and increased taxes would be imposed upon them in order to meet the cost of financing the recovery program. He expressed the hope that the taxpayers would bear the new tax burdens cheerfully in the knowledge that their money was being spent for the relief of suffering. He promised that every effort would be made to assure an equitable distribution of the tax burden, so that it would not weigh too heavily on any particular sector of the tax-paying public.[12]

The next day the new governor presented his program to the joint session of the legislature. He informed the legislators that he had organized several committees to study various aspects of the state government and that he had contracted with the Brookings Institution to advise the committees and report on their findings. Because this report would not be completed in time for consideration by the regular session, Marland proposed that revenue measures be enacted which would last only until the end of the following fiscal year, at which time the recommendations of the committees could be taken into account for an efficient solution to the state's problems. He reminded the legislators that the state would soon be responsible for the relief of about 150,000 individuals who were to be dropped from the federal relief rolls. He labeled the solution of the unemployment dilemma as the greatest task faced by the people. He urged the coordination of state and national relief programs, particularly in the area of public works, to relieve unemployment.

The governor recommended to the legislature the establishment and support of several state boards to coordinate the activities of the state in its effort to counteract the depression. Foremost among these was a state planning board which was to develop and coordinate plans for the effective use of the natural, agricultural, industrial, and human resources of the state. A flood control board was proposed to deal with the problems of flood control, soil erosion, irrigation, and reforestation. To aid in the resettlement and financing of homes for the many thousands who were homeless, he suggested a housing board, and a new industries board to encourage and direct the establishment of new industries in Oklahoma. He also called for a highway board, and suggested that members of the last four named boards be named ex-officio members of the state planning board in order to coordinate activities. In asking for these boards, Marland also submitted his request for appropriations for them.

Governor Marland also proposed emergency revenue measures to provide funds for his program. An increase of one cent per gallon in the gasoline tax was to finance the operation of the highway board. A severance tax of two cents per barrel on crude petroleum and two cents per thousand cubic feet on natural gas was to provide funds for the other four boards. To

Public work projects such as this served the dual purpose of providing employment and conserving the soil, solving two of the most pressing problems in Oklahoma during the Marland administration (Oklahoma Historical Society).

enhance the general revenue fund of the state, he proposed additional emergency taxes on incomes, inheritances, insurance premiums, cigarettes, salaries, and rent incomes. In order to raise revenue to meet the relief problem, he advocated a 3 percent tax on sales and services, two-thirds of the money to go for relief and one-third for the support of schools. He concluded his message by urging the enactment of his emergency proposals "in the name of suffering humanity."[13]

Marland was not as fortunate with the implementation of his New Deal as President Roosevelt had been in his early days in office. The New Deal did not come to Oklahoma in a whirlwind of rubber-stamped legislation similar to the "One Hundred

Days" of Roosevelt's administration. Marland's program, and particularly the monetary demands it placed on the state, brought heavy criticism to bear on him. His proposals for raising revenue touched very economic interest in the state, thereby fulfilling his promise of an equitable distribution of taxes, but this also meant that opposition to increased taxes would come from every sector of economic activity in the state. Business interests opposed the increased sales tax and the proposal for heavier taxes on oil production was not welcomed by the oil interests. As a former giant in the oil industry, Marland was aware of how much the producers of oil could afford to pay, and he felt it was time the wealthy oil interests began repaying the state for their good fortune and assist in shouldering a larger portion of the burden along with the other taxpayers.

His experience as a wealthy businessman and humanitarian during his heyday with the Marland Oil Company influenced his actions as governor. He had promised a businesslike administration of government and sought to keep this pledge by the establishment of boards to deal with specific problem areas and the use of economic planning to conteract the depression. His charitable spirit, exhibited by his generosity with his own wealth during the 1920s, was carried into office with him. The programs and plans he suggested were, he felt, needed and approved of by the people. Marland's generosity, however, was not shared by many Oklahomans, already under the pinch of hard times, who realized that the New Deal would be expensive if put into operation. Their concern was relayed to their representatives in the state legislature and, as a result, the legislators were not willing to follow Marland's program without careful consideration of the possible consequences of their actions.[14]

Marland became dismayed at the slow pace at which his proposals received consideration by the legislature. At the close of the sixth week of the legislative session, the only measure proposed by the governor which had passed both houses was a three cent per pack tax on cigarettes. The governor, alarmed at the prospect of his program being blocked, appeared before a joint caucus of both houses and appealed to the legislators to push consideration of his emergency proposals. He emphasized the need for the establishment of the boards which he had recommended, particularly the planning board, in order that the federal government would realize that Oklahoma was willing to work to solve its problems and cooperate with the federal recovery program. The necessity for federal matching funds for relief and public work projects was a dominant factor in the governor's desire to push the state program of recovery operations. With the aid of these matching funds, the state would be able to pursue recovery activities which it could not otherwise afford.[15]

The snail's pace in state legislative action impeding the progress of the Marland program was due primarily to the conservatism of the house of representatives. The leader of the conservative element was the speaker of the house, Leon C. Phillips. The fiery, cigar-chewing legislator defended his opposition to extensive appropriations by asserting that the legislature was following the will of the people. Referring to Marland's program, Phillips stated that the house of representatives was prepared to provide for the destitute but at the same time was "consevative enough to save the state from the hallucinations of dreamers." Phillips proposed to take care of the necessities of the state and then consider the governor's new proposals in light of the state's ability to pay for them. These necessities, according to Phillips, included the balancing of the state budget, providing for the necessary operating expenses of the state government, providing relief for those unable to work, and supporting the common schools.[16]

Marland also encountered opposition in the state senate early in his administrarion. The conflict arose over the question of senate confirmation of executive appointments. Members of the senate balked at approving Marland's appointees because they felt that the senate should have a voice in the selection of state officers instead of merely approving or disapproving the choices of the governor. The plums of patronage could in this manner be retained in the senate, thereby increasing the influence of that body and its members. The senators also complained that in selecting appointees, Marland was not distributing his choices evenly throughout the various sections of the state. Most of his initial appointments had been men from Kay and Oklahoma counties, men with whom he was familiar. The difficulties were resolved as the session progressed, however, and the senate swung into line behind the governor and supported his program for the remainder of the session.[17]

Governor Marland's continuing exasperation with the failure of the legislature to enact his measures was demonstrated when, on March 8, 1935, he appealed directly to the people of the state for their support. In two speeches broadcast over a statewide radio hookup, he reminded the people of the mandate he had received by his election to follow the national recovery program of President Roosevelt. He attacked the members of the Oklahoma House of Representatives for blocking his and, in effect, the president's plan for helping the state. He praised the Oklahoma Senate for its cooperation in his behalf but charged that the members of the house were acting under the influence of special interest groups and tax dodgers who sought to "deprive their fellow citizens of any share of the state's great abundance." He also lashed out at the state press for its lack of concern for the suffering and for keeping the public in apathy. Marland called on the people to write their state representatives and demonstrate their support for him.[18]

While Marland was admonishing the legislature for its failure to act, a crisis arose concerning the relief situation. The federal relief allotment had been reduced and the distress caused by this precipitated a hunger march in protest. A crowd of more than 300 hungry and jobless people gathered at the Pittsburg County Courthouse in McAlester, protesting the lack of relief funds and claiming that they would not leave until their demands were met. Governor Marland dispatched two truckloads of rations from the Oklahoma National Guard commissary to feed the protesters. He stated that due to the bottleneck in the legislature he had no relief funds at his disposal and, therefore, sending the rations to feed the people was the best he could do. The legislature had passed a measure creating a state welfare board, but had not yet passed measures to provide the necessary funds for relief.

The McAlester hunger marchers wanted relief, not temporary rations, so the two truckloads of food were left untouched by the crowd. A committee of fourteen of the marchers called on Governor Marland in Oklahoma City to explain the situation and plead for assistance. Marland told the committee that he would be unable to help them unless the legislature approved his recovery measures. The committee remained in Oklahoma City to observe the legislature in session. Spurred into action by the watchful eyes and the emergency situation, the senate speedily approved a bill appropriating $600,000 for emergency relief for the last two weeks in March, 1935. The funds were to be distrubuted by the federal relief administration, as the administrative facilities for state relief would not be operable until April 1. While the house was considering raising the appropriation to demonstrate its willingness to help, the federal relief allotment was received and the issue was dropped.[19]

Despite Marland's appeals, opposition continued in the house of representatives and the Marland package emerged at the end of the legislative session considerably altered. The legislature appropriated $2.5 million for relief, half of the sum proposed by the governor. The creation of the housing and new industries boards was not approved. The Oklahoma Planning and Resources Board and the Oklahoma Flood Control and Conservation Board were both appproved, but with accompanying appropriations for their operation of only a fraction of the amount suggested by Governor Marland. The sales tax remained at the old rate of 1 percent although it was expanded to include several services as well as gross sales. The one cent gasoline tax and the insurance premium tax also failed to be adopted.

The governor did not suffer a complete defeat of his program, however. The administration saw portions of its plan enacted into law despite the attrition in the legislature. Taxes on incomes, inheritances, cigarettes, and gross production of oil, along with the expanded sales and service tax, provided additional sources of revenue for the state government. The state planning and flood control boards, although limited by funds, offered a system through which state problems could be studied and a plan of action permitting closer cooperation with

Governor Marland proposed the establishment of a conservation board to deal with severe erosion problems such as on this Oklahoma farm (Oklahoma Historical Society).

the federal government in efforts to bring about recovery. The legislature also appropriated $8.2 million yearly for the support of common schools. The governor had at least obtained a foothold for climbing toward his goal of economic recovery and prosperity for Oklahoma.[20]

Marland was far from satisfied with the portion of his program which survived the legislative trimming. In a speech at a banquet of the Comanche County League of Young Democrats in Lawton on May 16, 1935, he denounced Phillips and the other members of the legislature for their failure to put into effect the program for action overwhelmingly approved the previous November by the people of Oklahoma. He maintained that Oklahoma Democrats had been "cruelly betrayed by your own house of representatives." He stated that if the people did not want his program, then he did not want the job of governor. He proposed to submit measures to the people for approval by special election. Accusing the members of the house of not representing the true feelings of their constituents, he proposed that "the people must pass laws until representatives are elected in a year and a half." He rejected the excuses offered by the legislators who said that their constituents did not want to pay for his program, telling the people that "you know you can't get something for nothing." He called on the people to help him strive for the goal of social security for Oklahomans.[21]

Governor Marland did not feel that the relief and social security measures passed by the legislature were sufficient to meet the needs of the state. The legislature, shortly before adjourning, had called for a special election to be held on September 24, 1935, to consider four referendum proposals. Marland favored placing an initiative measure on the ballot to provide for old-age pensions. The initiative measure was held up by hearings on the adequacy of the petitions, so in order to have the measure voted on, the governor placed it on the ballot by proclamation. It was approved by the voters, but was declared void in February, 1936, because of the governor's action in placing it on the ballot. Marland also initiated a measure which appropriated an additional $2.5 million for relief purposes. It provided for $1.5 million in relief until June 30, 1936, and $1 million for the following fiscal year. This was approved by the voters in a special election on December 17, 1935. It was passed primarily by the votes of people affected by relief with a vital personal interest in increased relief payments. The passage of the measure by a comparatively light voter turnout directly concerned with its success led to criticism in the state about the abuse of the initiative process of legislation which allowed minority rule. It also increased Marland's popularity as a chief executive who had the interests and welfare of underprivileged people at heart.[22]

Beginning the second year of his administration, Marland planned to continue efforts to bring more New Deal procedures to Oklahoma and outlined programs for the consideration of the next state legislative session. He emphasized social security legislation, continuation of certain taxes passed by the previous legislature, public work programs, relief for the unemployed by rural rehabilitation and subsistence homesteads, and state assistance in meeting the problems of agriculture. He also planned to initiate an old-age pension measure to replace the one declared void, along with an initiated increase in the sales tax to provide revenue for the pensions.[23]

Governor Marland astonished political observers in February, 1936, by announcing his candidacy for the United States Senate seat held by veteran Oklahoma statesman, Thomas P. Gore. This marked the first time that an Oklahoma governor had sought this position while still in office. Marland based his campaign for the United States Senate on a platform of cooperation with President Roosevelt, the same platform that had swept him into the governor's mansion two years earlier. Marland's opponents in seeking the nomination of the Democratic Party were, in addition to the incumbent Gore, Fifth District United States Congressman Joshua B. Lee and the candidate who supported the Townsend Pension Plan, Gomer Smith.

Marland placed a surprising second in the July 7, 1936, primary behind the highly popular Lee. Gore and Smith were eliminated from contention and the stage was set for a runoff primary battle between Marland and Lee. Marland chose to continue his bid despite Lee's margin of more than 40,000 votes in the first election, hoping to draw strength from the supporters of the two eliminated contenders, particularly the Smith pension plan group. The bid failed when Lee won the runoff primary by an overwhelming margin. The July, 1936, primary was evidence that Oklahoma was in favor of the New Deal, as Lee also proposed to cooperate with President Roosevelt. The results were viewed not so much as a repudiation of Marland but as an endorsement of Lee, and Oklahoma retained her New Deal pilot. Marland did, however, suffer from voter rejection because of his use of the state administrative machinery and employees to help finance and further his candidacy.[24]

There were several interesting and significant sidelights to the Marland senatorial campaign. He had announced his opposition to the legislators who had opposed him in the 1935 legislative session and he was paying close attention to the developing legislative races with an eye on the organization of the next session. One of the leading administration supporters in the senate, James C. Nance, had switched his campaign to the house in order to strengthen the administration position and hopefully displace Phillips as speaker. Both Nance and Phillips won their races and both factions began aligning support in anticipation of the impending struggle for control of the house. The July, 1936, primary also saw the adoption of the old-age pension and 2 percent sales tax which had been initiated by Governor Marland and signified a large step in his efforts to achieve social security for his fellow Oklahomans.[25]

Following the election of a new legislature in November, 1936, the Democratic members met to decide on the organization of the leadership of the house of representatives. A close struggle took place between the forces of Phillips and the administration forces led by J. T. Daniel. Daniel received the powerful position of speaker when Phillips withdrew from the fray to spare his supporters embarrassment under the watchful eyes of Governor Marland. Nance was selected to be floor leader and control of the house was firmly in the hands of supporters of the governor.[26]

No longer intimidated by the probability of a struggle with the Phillips faction in the house of representatives, Governor Marland called a special session of the legislature for the consideration of matters he felt would not wait until the opening of the regular session in January, 1937. He submitted emergency proposals for dealing with drought, welfare, unemployment, and homestead tax exemption, along with several other matters needing the attention of the state government. The special session approved approximately half of Marland's proposals, including relief appropriations and unemployment insurance, and dispensed with much of the confusion of organization which would ordinarily occupy the opening days of the regular session.[27]

The regular session of the legislature convened on January 5, 1937, the day after the adjournment of the special session. Governor Marland began his message to the final legislative session of his administration by stating that conditions were little better in Oklahoma than when he took office. He spoke of the need for social security legislation and for the advancement of the social and political system to meet the new problems facing the state. He emphasized the questions of drought and farm tenancy, and the erosion of the natural resources of the state. He stated his belief that complaining taxpayers did not take the proper view of taxes and realize that the benefits received from their tax dollars made these dollars better spent than any others they would spend. Marland repeated his pledge to work with the federal government and called for generous appropriations to be made to meet the needs of the state. He urged the legislators to enact sufficient revenue measures to finance the extensive appropriations in order to keep the budget balanced. He pledged his cooperation in meeting the needs of the state throughout the session.[28]

In calling for generous appropriations, Governor Marland had not outlined a specific plan for legislative action. He preferred instead to rely on the wisdom of the legislators to enact a program suitable to meet the existing situation. The battle with the 1935 legislature had taught him not to lay all his cards on the table and have his plans attacked by the press and special interest groups. But without a definite plan of action, the legislature did not proceed in an efficient or assertive manner toward enacting emergency legislation. Governor Marland had to intervene and urge that the legislators pass emergency proposals before considering the many minor and local bills. Responding to the gentle prodding of the governor to enact social security legislation, the legislature complied with his request for generous appropriations with a record setting appropriation for the next two years, but was hesitant in passing sufficient revenue measures to maintain the balance of the state budget. Marland, foreseeing the likelihood of a huge state deficit, asked for authority to trim appropriations on a quarterly basis to meet existing revenues, but his request was denied. Both the legislature and the governor drew criticism for their failure to follow a plan to keep the state out of debt.[29]

Instead of being content to serve out his term of office, Marland sought to continue in the service of Oklahoma by once again announcing his candidacy for the United States Senate in 1938. This time he faced incumbent Senator Elmer Thomas and Gomer Smith. The campaign was highlighted by a visit to the state of President Roosevelt three days before the primary. Roosevelt spoke in Oklahoma City on July 9, 1938, making little reference to the primary campaign, although he mentioned "my old friend Senator Thomas" in what was taken by many observers to be an endorsement of Senator Thomas.[30] He did not mention the role of Governor Marland in helping to carry out his New Deal policies, saying only that "we are developing a national policy in regard to the oil resources of the nation, and your governor has given great assistance toward that end."[31] Marland refused to admit that the president had endorsed Senator Thomas, claiming that "he didn't put his arm around anybody."[32] But Marland lost the primary to Senator Thomas. The lack of endorsement by the leader he tried to follow seemed to reflect the decline in Marland's political fortunes.[33]

Marland's administration also brought about many other improvements in the state. He worked constantly for the conservation of natural resouces, such as encouraging reforestation and the use of erosion fighting techniques. He also took the lead in the creation and support of the Interstate Oil Compact, through which the oil producing states cooperated for the conservation and prudent marketing of valuable oil and gas resources. He was responsible for the creation of the Oklahoma Department of Public Safety and its highway patrol. He consistently urged improvement and expansion of state institutions such as prisons, orphanages, and mental health facilities. His support of education led to increased appropriations and improved conditions in Oklahoma schools. But his foremost contribution to the state was the energetic pursuit of achieving social security for Oklahomans who were suffering from the collapse of the normal order of economic activity. His

actions in urging the cooperation of state and federal governments helped bring aid and jobs to many who would otherwise
have been left with little hope for economic survival.[34]

After leaving the office of governor in January, 1939, to Leon
C. Phillips, his persistent opponent, Marland returned to his
home in Ponca City and devoted his energy to the reorganization
of the Marland Oil Company. He made an unspectacular return
to politics in 1940 when he sought the Democratic nomination
for the United States House of Representatives, but ill health
forced him to curtail his campaigning and he was soundly
defeated. His health continued to worsen and he died of a heart
ailment on October 3, 1941. He was buried in a mausoleum in
Odd Fellows Cemetery in Ponca City, where the symbols of his
generosity and kindness abound and serve as a lasting
monument to his memory.[35]

Marland served the state well during his public career.
Humanitarianism dominated his actions on behalf of his fellow
Oklahomans and perhaps prevented him from being the expert
in political manupulation which might have moved his program
through the legislature in its entirety. He seemed at times
unable to believe that the people would let short-term financial
considerations such as taxes destroy the possibility for long-
term benefits for everyone. He observed the disorder and
distress caused by the depression and sought to devote his
efforts to help the state recover economically. He desired to use
the state government as the instrument by which he could best
aid the largest number of people in the most ways possible. He
sought to follow the example of President Roosevelt's New Deal
and exerted his influence to urge the utmost cooperation with
the national program so that Oklahomans could receive the
maximum benefit possible.

The setbacks suffered by Marland in carrying out his economic
recovery program in Oklahoma were due to disagreement over
the nature of the government's taxation role. Marland received
considerable criticism for his use of state taxation to help
achieve his economic recovery goals. His motivation was not
selfish, but was designed to help Oklahomans help themselves.
Although much of his economic recovery program was not put
into effect, his efforts brought relief and hope to many

Governor Marland's energetic efforts to fight the Great Depression brought relief to thousands of Oklahomans forced to live in shacks such as this on a bare subsistence level (Oklahoma Historical Society).

thousands of Oklahomans and started the state on the road to economic recovery. The portions of his program put into action were a giant step toward economic recovery and brought about considerable improvement in the state. The impact of Marland's actions can best be perceived when his accomplishments are compared to the situation in the state as it would have been without his energetic efforts to bring the New Deal to Oklahoma.

ENDNOTES

[1] *Congressional Record*, 73rd Cong., 2nd sess., p. 7354.
[2] *Oklahoma City Times* (Oklahoma City), July 16, 1934, p. 7, July 17, 1934, p. 4.
[3] *Ibid.*, July 18, 1934, p. 12, July 19, 1934, p. 14.

[4] E. W. Marland, *My Experience with the Money Trust* (Enid: Enid Press, 1932), pp. 3, 4, 5.

[5] *Daily Oklahoman* (Oklahoma City), June 8, 1921, p. 4; *Ponca City News* (Ponca City), April 23, 1930, p. 1; *Oklahoma City Times*, August 4, 1934, p. 3.

[6] Marland, *My Experience with the Money Trust*, pp. 6-14.

[7] *Ponca City News*, November 10, 1932, p. 1; *Congressional Record*, 73rd Cong., 1st sess., pp. 2932-2934, 2940-2941, 3808-3810, 5698-5699; *ibid.*, 2nd sess., pp. 6109-6111, 7080-7082, 7353-7354.

[8] *Harlow's Weekly*, Vol. XLIII, No. 1 (July 7, 1934), p. 6; *Daily Oklahoman*, July 6, 1934, p. 1.

[9] *Ponca City News*, November 7, 1934, p. 1; *Harlow's Weekly*, Vol. XLIII, No. 20 (December 1, 1934), p. 8.

[10] *Daily Oklahoman*, July 1, 1934, p. 16A; *Harlow's Weekly*, Vol. XLIV, No. 4 (January 26, 1935), pp. 2-3.

[11] *Daily Oklahoman*, November 12, 1934, p. 1934, p. 1, November 13, 1934, p. 1, January 6, 1935, p. 1.

[12] *Ibid.*, January 15, 1935, pp. 1-2; E. W. Marland, *Inaugural Address of Governor E. W. Marland* (Oklahoma City: Central Printing Company, 1935), pp. 1-7.

[13] Oklahoma House, *Journal of the House of Representatives, Fifteenth Legislature, Regular Session, 1935*, 2 vols., (Oklahoma City: Leader Press, 1935), Vol. I, pp. 237-245.

[14] *Harlow's Weekly*, Vol. XLIV, No. 3 (January 19, 1935), pp. 15-16; *Daily Oklahoman*, January 6, 1935, p. 1, May 18, 1935, p. 2.

[15] *Harlow's Weekly*, Vol. XLIV, No. 7 (February 16, 1935), pp. 4-5.

[16] *Daily Oklahoman*, February 15, 1935, p. 1.

[17] *Ibid.*, January 18, 1935, p. 1; *Harlow's Weekly*, Vol. XLIV, No. 4 (January 26, 1935), pp. 2-3, Vol. XLIV, No. 16 (May 4, 1935), p. 2.

[18] *Daily Oklahoman*, March 9, 1935, pp. 1-2.

[19] *Ibid.*, March 10, 1935, p. 1, March 11, 1935, p. 4, March 12, 1935, p. 1, March 13, 1935, p. 1, March 17, 1935, p. 1.

[20] *Harlow's Weekly*, Vol. XLIV, No. 16 (May 4, 1935), pp. 4-5.

[21] *Daily Oklahoman*, May 17, 1935, pp. 1-2.

[22] *Ibid.*, September 18, 1935, p. 1, September 26, 1935, p. 1, December 18, 1935, p. 1, February 19, 1936, p. 1; *Harlow's Weekly*, Vol. XLV, No. 24 (December 21, 1935), pp. 3, 13, 14, Vol. XLV, No. 25 (December 28, 1935), p. 5.

[23] *Daily Oklahoman*, February 16, 1936, p. 1, February 19, 1936, p. 1.

[24] *Harlow's Weekly*, Vol. XLVII, No. 1 (July 4-11, 1936), p. 5, Vol. XLVII, No. 4 (August 1, 1936), pp. 3-4; *Daily Oklahoman*, February 23, 1936, p. 1, July 8, 1936, p. 1, July 29, 1936, p. 1.

[25] *Daily Oklahoman*, July 8, 1936, p. 1, July 9, 1936, p. 1.

[26] *Harlow's Weekly*, Vol. XLVII, No. 18 (November 7, 1936), pp. 10-11; *Daily Oklahoman*, November 6, 1936, p. 1.

[27] Oklahoma House, *Journal of the House of Representatives, Sixteenth Legislature, First Extraordinary Session, 1937* (Oklahoma City: Leader Press, 1937), pp. 15-18; *Harlow's Weekly*, Vol. XLVII, No. 26 (January 2, 1937), pp. 9-11; *Daily Oklahoman*, January 5, 1937, pp. 1-2.

[28] Oklahoma House, *Journal of the House of Representatives, Sixteenth Legislature, Regular Session 1937*, 2 vols. (Oklahoma City: Leader Press, 1937), Vol. I, pp. 40-55.

[29] *Ibid.*, p. 51; *Daily Oklahoman*, January 24, 1937, p. 1; *Harlow's Weekly*, Vol. XLVII, No. 46 (May 15, 1937), pp. 9, 10, 11, 13.

[30] *Daily Oklahoman*, July 10, 1938, pp. 1-2.

[31] *Ibid.*

[32] *Ibid.*, p. 18A.

[33] *Ibid.*, July 13, 1938, p. 1.

[34] Oklahoma House, *Journal of the House of Representatives, Seventeenth Legislature, Regular Session, 1939*, 2 vols. (Oklahoma City: Leader Press, 1939), Vol. I, pp. 37-56.

[35] *Ponca City News*, September 25, 1939, p. 1, June 19, 1940, p. 8, July 10, 1040, p. 2, October 3, 1941, p. 1; *Tulsa Tribune* (Tulsa), October 6, 1941, p. 9.

Leon Chase Phillips

Governor of Oklahoma, 1939-1943

by Sara L. Bernson

Leon Chase Phillips

For two years Governor Leon Chase Phillips had battled against President Franklin D. Roosevelt and the New Deal. In 1940 Phillips found himself head of the Democratic Party in Oklahoma when there was talk of a third term for Roosevelt. Phillips wanted to send an uncommitted delegation to the Democratic National Convention, despite congressional support for a third term. When Phillips led the delegation to Chicago, Illinois, in July, its instructions were to support Roosevelt for a third term if he so desired. Once it was obvious that President Roosevelt wanted a third term, the Oklahoma delegation gave him its complete backing—except for Phillips. When the convention erupted into a demonstration for Roosevelt, Phillips watched in silence. As demonstrators marched by holding state banners, Phillips held an Oklahoma banner in his hand. Phillips presented a physical dare to anyone who even thought of trying to take the banner from him. Roosevelt received the nomination, but Phillips had no intention of supporting him.[1]

Phillips probably inherited his independent streak. He was born on December 9, 1890, on a farm in Worth County, Missouri. His parents, Rufus and Bertha Phillips, were rural

Governor Phillips led the Oklahoma delegation at the Democratic National Convention in Chicago in 1940. He did not support President Franklin D. Roosevelt for a third term and he did not join in the demonstration following Roosevelt's nomination (Oklahoma Publishing Company).

farmers. In 1892 his father moved to the newly opened Cheyenne-Arapaho land in Oklahoma Territory and claimed a quarter section west of Clinton. The family later traveled by train to their new home. Within a few years Rufus Phillips and a neighbor started the first school in the community so that the Phillips children and others could receive an education close to home. In 1905 the family moved to the town of Arapaho so Rufus could practice law. Leon attended the public grade school in the town, and graduated from high school in three years. While attending school, Phillips decided he wanted to be a Methodist Church minister. This interest in religion was probably due to the influence of his mother, whose heritage was Pennsylvania Dutch.[2]

In order to support his religious training, Phillips decided to teach. He attended Southwestern State Teachers College in Weatherford briefly, and took a teaching position in Custer County in the fall of 1908. During the Christmas vacation, however, he caught pneumonia while baling hay. He was forced to resign from his job and remain at home, ill, until the following July. While recuperating, Phillips chose to study for the Methodist Church ministry at Epworth University, presently Oklahoma City University, in Oklahoma City. For the first year, he supported his studies by cleaning the kitchen and dining room of the school. The second year he received a scholarship from the Oklahoma City Federated Women's Club and was able to put more time into school activities, such as the debating team and literary society.[3]

In the winter of 1912, after two years of theological study, Phillips decided against the ministry as a career and turned to law. In September, 1912, Phillips entered the University of Oklahoma law school. He paid for his education from savings the first year and by selling livestock the second year; his father paid for the third year. It was during these years at the University of Oklahoma that Phillips first became active in politics. He was named president of the student council and was elected best all-around student his final year. He joined the law school's football team, and due to the color of his hair he was dubbed "Red," a nickname he used throughout his life. He met

Myrtle Ellenberger, a student at the university, and they became engaged in June, 1913. The wedding was scheduled to take place soon after Phillips's graduation. The plans, nevertheless, were delayed when Phillips hurt his stomach while helping his classmates paint a smokestack as a joke; the couple finally married on June 19, 1916.[4]

After the wedding, Phillips moved to Okemah, where he formed a law partnership with Ural A. Rowe, a friend from law school. They selected lawsuits in which they strongly believed, and won twenty-nine out of their first thirty cases. World War I, however, interrupted the law practice of Phillips. He entered officer training school at Camp Taylor, Kentucky, in April, 1918, but again his plans were changed due to illness. He contracted influenza and was discharged in December, 1918.[5]

Phillips returned to law practice in Okemah, and within a few years he became active in the local Democratic Party. He served as a nonpartisan member on the city school board from 1922 to 1926. He was appointed secretary of the Okfuskee County Election Board in 1926 after successfully representing election officials in the federal court on charges of denying the vote to blacks. Phillips served as secretary until 1932, when he ran as the Democratic candidate for the Oklahoma House of Representatives.[6] By the summer of 1933, Phillips had established a reputation, said a newspaper reporter, as "one of the most dynamic and forceful members of the house."[7]

Phillips introduced legislation on an inheritance tax, an insurance fund, a reduction in county officials' salaries, and a homestead tax-exemption law, the last of which failed. It was at this time that he first introduced the idea of coordinating higher education in Oklahoma, an idea that he would later support as governor. He was unopposed for reelection in 1934, and during his second term he ran for speaker of the house of representatives. He won despite opposition from three other contenders and Governor Ernest W. Marland. He served a third term, beginning in 1936, but lost in his bid for speaker of the house of representatives due to conflicts with Marland over spending.[8]

While still in the house of representatives, Phillips began thinking of running for governor. He talked to political leaders as well as suspected and declared candidates. If he found someone he could support, he would not feel the need to run. He discovered, however, that he could not support any of the contenders, and in January, 1938, declared himself a candidate in the Democratic Party primary for governor. His announcement was made in Weleetka, at a party with a motif of red. At this gathering he promised to put the Oklahoma Highway Commission and the Oklahoma Tax Commission on strict budgets.[9] He declared that with an "elimination of excess baggage . . . and with strict economy" he would "pay the exisiting deficit . . . and provide for all the necessities of government without any increases of taxes."[10]

The platform of Phillips promised to limit the salaries and the number of state employees, and to place all state departments on strict budgets. He also said tht he would establish schools on a permanent basis, encourage progressive farm legislation, and assume power over pardons and paroles. He attacked his predecessors by saying he would take the Oklahoma Highway Commission and the Oklahoma Tax Commission "away from the corrupt politicians, to whom W. H. Murray delivered them in 1933."[11] He also stated that he would prevent relief and old-age pension funds from being "'gobbled up' by unnecessary white-collared swivel-chaired loafers who now honeycomb the administrative machinery."[12]

Phillips also reported that he would help reestablish condidence in the government of Oklahoma and respect for the Oklahoma Supreme Court. He declared that he would have "respect for and uphold the legislative branch of government."[13] During his announcement Phillips identified himself with President Roosevelt by ending a tribute to him "by holding aloft a framed picture of Mr. Roosevelt and asking that the audience stand to express its respect and admiration [for Roosevelt]."[14] The popularity of the announcement of Phillips could be seen by the attendance at the meeting and by the fact that many of his legislative colleagues came to the ceremony.

In the primary campaign Phillips's main opponents were William H. Murray, running for a second term as governor, and William S. Key, former head of the Works Progress Administration in Oklahoma. Though the contest was among three men, the voting broke down into pro-Murray and anti-Murray voters, with the latter splitting their support between Phillips and Key. From the beginning the candidates tried to appeal to special interest groups. Phillips and Key fought for the church vote and the education bloc. Early in the race Phillips received the support of labor because he had introduced a minimum wage and hour law in the house of representatives. He also received the backing of a majority of newspapers when his campaign opened with one of the largest newspaper displays in the state's history.[15]

Throughout the summer of 1938 Phillips campaigned on a platform of fiscal responsibility and relief for the needy. Early polls predicted Key the winner, but Phillips intensified his effort in eastern Oklahoma, which strongly supported Key, and in urban areas. In July, President Roosevelt planned a trip to Oklahoma, and people speculated whether he would comment on the gubernatorial race. Though he made a negative comment about Murray, Roosevelt did not declare support for any of the candidates, though Key expected his endorsement. When the results of the primary were announced on July 13, 1938, it was clear that the extra effort of Phillips was successful. He took the lead from the beginning, and finally won a majority by 3,100 votes, one of the closest gubernatorial primaries until that time in Oklahoma history.[16]

Once Phillips received the Democratic nomination, there was little doubt that he would defeat his Republican opponent, Ross Rizley, in the November general election. He ran on the same issues during the election as he had in the primary. He campaigned against patronage, especially in the old-age pension system. He refused to name any appointments until after the general election, and warned state legislators against making promises that he would not keep. One difference in his campaign was his attitude toward President Roosevelt. Though Phillips had previously supported him, after he secured the nomination, he did not mention the New Deal.[17]

Phillips and Jesse Chipman watch the returns of the Democratic gubernatorial primary in 1938. Phillips won by one of the smallest margins in Oklahoma history (Oklahoma Publishing Company).

On election day Phillips voted at his hometown of Okemah. As election returns came in, it was no surprise that Phillips had won by a large margin. He ran strongly in all areas of the state except the northwest, Rizley's home territory. Though he would not take office until January, 1939, Phillips immediately became active in the problems of the governorship. He announced that he was not a New Dealer, saying "I'm one of those individuals who believes that the head of the federal government should not interfere in state politics."[18] Within days after the election Phillips traveled to Washington, D.C., to investigate problems between the state and federal governments over old-age pensions. He wanted to establish his control over such federal programs in Oklahoma.[19]

Governor Phillips in his inaugural address emphasized his opposition to excessive state spending and to the Red River Denison Dam (Oklahoma Publishing Company).

The inauguration of Phillips was on January 9, 1939; his first visit with the legislature, however, was earlier. Three days before taking the oath of office, Phillips visited the Oklahoma Senate and the Oklahoma House of Representatives, an unprecedented action by a governor-elect. Though rain was expected on inauguration day, sunshine greeted the crowd of 10,000 that had gathered to hear the inaugural speech of Phillips. He promised to eliminate state government extravagance, pledging to decrease the number of state employees. He declared his opposition to the Red River Denison Dam, then being constructed by the federal government. Two days after his inauguration, Phillips addressed a joint session of the state legislature. He suggested that the lawmakers should not make appropriations above estimated revenues. He also continued his attack against the Red River Denison Dam. Thus, by the end of his second day in office, Phillips had outlined the issues of his administration: fiscal responsibility and federal construction within the state.[20]

If Phillips was to keep his promises, he would need tight control over the legislature. One of the first test cases of his control was the reorganization of the Oklahoma Highway Commission. He desired to reduce the number of commissioners by one, and he wanted the governor to have the power to remove a member. The senate gave its complete support to the plan, and the house of representatives also quickly passed the bill. Phillips signed it on January 11, 1939, and it became the first law enacted during his administration. Though the old commission had accumulated a debt of more than $4.7 million, the new commission would have to operate on a cash basis. The quick passage of the act proved that the legislature was willing to support the governor in his attempts to restore fiscal stability to the state.[21]

Though the reorganization of the Oklahoma Highway Commission seemed to promise cooperation between the governor and legislature, the lawmakers kept some of their independence. In the attempt of Phillips to balance the budget, he wanted state taxes collected on time. He was against any extension for paying ad valorem taxes for 1937 and prior years. Despite threats of a veto, the house of representatives passed a bill which extended the deadline for payment of taxes and waived all penalties and interest on outstanding taxes. The senate also passed the bill, and Phillips signed it despite his personal feelings.[22]

The legislature's second attempt to assert its independence involved patronage. The governor wanted to reduce the number of gasoline inspectors from 140 to 20. The inspectors, according to a political commentator, had long "been a pillar of political power" within the state.[23] The senate defeated a bill to reduce the number, but the house of representatives passed the bill, showing its support for Phillips. The senate then gave in to pressures, and passed the bill reorganizing and reducing the number of inspectors. The bill was not only important for reducing patronage, but also for encouraging a balanced budget.[24]

In addition to these test cases of Phillips's control, his power can also be seen in many smaller issues. He had campaigned on reducing the number of state employees, and the legislature was willing to help. Its phone bill was cut by $5,000; the number of house of representatives employees was reduced by approximately 25 percent; the practice of typing copies of the legislative journal was also stopped, at a savings of $15,000. The sales tax was extended for two years, providing extra funds for a balanced budget. Though strongly supported by legislators, a provision for free textbooks for school children was rejected after Phillips denounced the plan.[25]

In addition, the legislature also helped Phillips in his urgent need to reorganize the Oklahoma Public Welfare Commission. The group was at odds with the federal social security board over the administration of funds. The federal government had cut off funds, and hinted that the money would not be restored until a new commission was named. Though the problem had developed during the previous administration, Phillips had to solve it. In January, 1939, he demanded a report from the commission on its differences with the federal government, and declared that he would ask for resignations if necessary. Two members resigned, but at a meeting with the governor on January 12, five of the remaining seven members refused to quit until the federal government demanded their resignation. The Oklahoma House of Representatives supported Phillips by passing a resolution calling for the resignation of the commission, but Phillips still could not get the members to resign. With this new impasse the legislature called for a special election to consider a constitutional amendment. This would have voted the old commission out of existence and allowed Phillips to create a new one.[26]

In the meantime, state funds were running low and the Oklahoma Public Welfare Commission ordered the March, 1939, payments reduced by at least 50 percent. The chairman of the federal social security board then told Oklahoma's congressmen that funds would not be restored until the problem was settled. Due to mounting pressure, all but four members of the welfare commission resigned. To add more pressure, the house of representatives in February had organized a special impeachment committee of the legislature to investigate the welfare commission. At an all-day meeting, two members agreed to resign if the federal government requested it. Phillips continued to apply pressure, and the remaining members started to resign. The last commissioner resigned in mid-February, when the impeachment investigative committee of the legislature passed a resolution commending the welfare commission for its resignation. After the appointment of a new commission, federal funding was restored.[27]

Though the legislature had tried to show its independence, it usually supported Phillips. One major area of difference, however, concerned the funding of common schools. Public schools had requested $12.8 million a year for the biennium, the same amount received for the previous two years. Phillips wanted to reduce the appropriation to $8 million and force local governments to collect taxes to support the schools. Though the Oklahoma Education Association supported the request, it finally accepted the $11.5 million a year that the senate and house of representatives agreed to appropriate. Phillips wanted a larger reduction, but he was satisfied that all departments would cooperate in trying to achieve a balanced budget.[28]

With the passage of the appropriation bills, the work of the 1939 legislature was completed. The end of legislative matters did not, however, mean a quiet year for Phillips. In 1939 the federal government was constructing two dams in Oklahoma. One was the Grand River Dam, the other was the Red River Denison Dam. The Grand River Dam began as a state project in 1935, but it had to borrow money from the federal government in 1937. The government had lent approximately $11.5 million and gave a grant of approximately $8.4 million to the state. By the time that Phillips became governor, the dam was near completion, but continued work was involved in a dispute between the state and federal governments. The state government wanted $889,275 for state property which would be flooded by the dam; the federal government wanted to pay

When Governor Phillip declared martial law to prevent the completion of the Grand River Dam, units of the Oklahoma National Guard were sent to enforce his proclamation (Oklahoma Publishing Company.)

$749,640. The conflict worsened when Phillips became tired of waiting for a settlement. On February 25, 1940, he declared that the dam would not be completed until the state received payment. He would order martial law and "use the national guard if necessary," he promised.[29] A few days later Phillips told local officials that the property of the Grand River Dam Authority was taxable.[30]

Phillips then carried out the threats. On March 13, 1940, martial law became effective at the dam site, and he ordered the Oklahoma National Guard to the dam. The troops were to allow construction to continue, but to prevent the closing of arch six, the only section still open. Phillips also received a temporary restraining order from a state judge preventing the closing of arch six. The federal government protested the use of state courts, and United States Senator Josh Lee of Oklahoma criticized Phillips in a speech to the United States Senate.[31] It was the consensus of citizens in the dam area that Phillips had "pulled a bust," a newspaper reporter observed, because they did not understand his opposition.[32]

On March 19, a federal court nullified the temporary restraining order, and issued its own restraining order against the use of Oklahoma National Guard troops to stop completion of the dam. Within a few days arch six was completed, and the water began rising in the 52,000-acre reservoir. Phillips refused to acknowledge defeat, left the Oklahoma National Guard troops at the dam, and took his case to court. He threatened to fire the board of directors of the Grand River Dam Authority, and the federal government countered by threatening to place the authority in receivership. Phillips won a moral victory in February, 1941, when the United States Supreme Court ruled that the lower federal court had acted improperly. The federal government placed the authority in receivership in December, 1941, but for national defense purposes and not because of its earlier threat.[33]

The controversy about the Red River Denison Dam was a state rights issue, according to Phillips. He claimed that the dam would not control floods, and that the main beneficiary of the power generated by the dam would be Texas. Although the Oklahoma public was split in its support of the dam, and although the Oklahoma delegation to the United States Congress backed the dam, Phillips took a stand against the federal government. He tried to sue to prevent the construction of the dam, but in February, 1940, the United States Supreme Court refused to hear his case. An oil strike in the dam area further complicated the issue by increasing the value of the land to be flooded, but a representative of the federal government said drilling would be no problem. After repeated attempts by Phillips to block the dam, settlement was made in December, 1941, and the dam was completed.[34]

Though Phillips's fights against the dams occupied some of his time from 1939 to 1941, the latter year was more important

Governor Phillips signing the legislative bill creating the Oklahoma State Regents for Higher Education. He is surrounded by the author of the bill and the appointees to the board. Left to right: Martin J. Phillips, James M. Staten, Lloyd R. Van Deventer, Earl E. Emerson, Charles G. Ozmun (author of the bill), Martin L. Frerichs, James T. Martin, Richard Martin, and William B. Hurst (Oklahoma Publishing Company).

for the meeting of the second biennial legislature of his term as governor. For this group of lawmakers, Phillips had planned a busy schedule. His main goal was a balanced budget. This meant new revenue sources and a constitutional amendment making a balanced budget mandatory. To obtain extra money, Phillips recommended reforming the tax laws and adding new ones, such as an amusement tax. He would also recommend reductions in appropriations.[35]

Early in the legislative session Phillips requested several constitutional amendments. One required a balanced budget. He desired a second amendment that would reorganize the state's institutions of higher education under one coordinating board of regents. He supported a third amendment guaranteeing the payment of old-age pensions. A special election would be held in March, 1941, for a vote on the amendments.[36]

Opposition to the balance budget amendment came basically

from the common school bloc. Dan Proctor, president of the Oklahoma Education Association, accused the governor of trying to achieve a balanced budget at the expense of the schools. The association, however, declared its support for the amendment if it would prohibit all earmarking of revenues except for those from the sales tax. Oklahoma Superintendent of Public Instruction Alvin L. Crable was also against the amendment. He protested that it would make the schools bear most of the burden, that it would make a nine-month school term almost impossible, and that it delegated legislative powers to the governor. As the special election drew nearer, Crable and some friends sent out 15,000 pamphlets against the amendment.[37]

To combat this opposition, Phillips appealed directly to the teachers. He warned that if the amendment was defeated there would be no extra funds for the schools, and he also promised higher salaries for teachers because the amendment would stabilize state financing. This would allow for a ten dollar a month raise. Phillips also requested a bill taking patronage away from Crable. Phillips received help in fighting the opposition. Both the Democratic and Republican parties supported the change, citizens formed committees to work for its passage, and in general taxpayers were happy with the amendment.[38]

The special election on the constitutional amendments was held on March 11, 1941. An unusually light voter turnout decided that the state would go on a cash basis. The balanced budget amendment passed by a two to one margin; the old-age pension amendment received a three to one victory; and the coordinating school board amendment passed by less than a two to one margin. The balanced budget amendment was to go into effect in July, 1941. This meant that the legislature would need to match appropriations with revenue for the next biennium.[39]

As a result of the special election, the legislature became unusually busy. One of its first acts was revenge against Crable; he was stripped of his patronage power. To fulfill the balanced budget amendment, the Oklahoma Board of Equalization had to estimate revenue for the next biennium, but the legislature knew that it had to raise revenue and also cut appropriations.[40]

Several new revenue bills were presented to the legislature. The gasoline tax was increased by one and one-half cents, bringing it to five and one-half cents on a gallon. The tax on cigarettes was raised from three to five cents on a package. The tax on the gross receipts of nonstate insurance companies was doubled. License tag fees were also raised. As a result of new taxes and expanded taxes, Oklahomans had to pay an extra $13 million in taxes. Though this extra revenue would help achieve a balanced budget, reductions in appropriations were also needed.[41]

All state institutions were expected to have reductions in their fundings. The number of state judicial districts was reduced by seven, which would provide a savings of $40,000 a year. The University of Oklahoma budget was reduced by approximately $800,000 a year. The Oklahoma Agricultural and Mechanical College request was cut by approximately $400,000 a year. Governmental departments had total budget reductions of approximately $1 million a year. Common schools also faced a cut in funds. Phillips wanted an appropriation of $8 million, but after much debate, a joint senate and house of representatives committee finally agreed on an appropriation of $8.6 million for the first year and $8.1 million for the second year. With agreement on aid to the common schools, the 1941 legislature finished its work.[42]

Although the legislature adjourned in May, 1941, Phillips had a year and one-half remaining of his term as governor. In March, 1941, a minor dispute had occurred when state officials took down Works Progress Administration signs from state food stamp offices. The same month Phillips took another stab at the federal government. At a convention in Chickasha, Phillips and the Washita Valley Improvement Association joined forces to attack a proposed federal dam on the Arkansas River. The project was, he declared, an "attempt to further abrogate our rights to develop and control our natural resources."[43] He blamed Oklahoma's congressmen of being afraid of Speaker of the House Sam Rayburn and for allowing the state to lose more than 100,000 acres of land for the Red River Denison Dam. A few months later he sent to the United States House of

The battleship Oklahoma *was capsized by the Japanese at Pearl Harbor, Hawaii Territory, on December 7, 1941. It is shown being refloated in 1943, but it sank in the Pacific Ocean in 1947 while being towed to California for scrap metal (Oklahoma Historical Society).*

Representatives Flood Control Committee a letter protesting two proposed dams in northeastern Oklahoma.[44]

Though Phillips had developed a reputation for opposing President Roosevelt, when it was necessary he could support him. With the bombing of Pearl Harbor, Hawaii Territory, Phillips moderated his antagonism towards Roosevelt. As governor, he gave total support to the World War II effort. On December 8, 1941, the day following the Pearl Harbor attack, Phillips issued a proclamation urging Oklahomans to remain calm. He warned that "our people must not give way to hysteria. . . . I advise you again to be cool, determined and patriotic."[45] He cautioned the public not to take justice into its own hands, and told them not "to constitute themselves courts, juries, and executioners."[46] Phillips announced that the state would waive use and sale taxes on defense contracts if requested to do so by the federal government. He also suggested using convicts as laborers to keep defense plants operating. He was quick to declare his support for the war and lend his help for United States victory.[47]

Another issue arose in December, 1941, that would occupy Phillips for the next year. State elections, including the one for governor, would be held in 1942. Phillips promised that he would stay out of the campaign, claiming it would be against a 1938 campaign pledge. He said that he would not interfere with the election or the Democratic Party. He announced, however, that no one could hold a state office and run for another state office at the same time. This policy caused E. W. Smartt, chairman of the Oklahoma Board of Public Affairs, to resign, due to his speculation about running for governor. Even though he quit, he decided against running for the office.[48]

It was obvious in early 1942 that the Democratic Party was turning against Phillips. In January, Oklahoma County elected Andrew Fraley as its party chairman, instead of the contender supported by Phillips. In February, anti-Phillips forces reelected France Paris as chairman of the Oklahoma Democratic Central Committee. When Phillips decided he would not attend the Oklahoma Washington Day Banquet, a Democratic Party function, Robert S. Kerr, general chairman of the event, accused him of "betraying . . . Democratic loyalty and fidelity."[49] Kerr announced his candidacy for governor in March, and he became the one man Phillips wanted defeated. In April, people thought Phillips was interfering in the campaign when Dr. Henry G. Bennett was not reelected president of Oklahoma Agricultural and Mechanical College. It seemed that Phillips wanted to force Bennett into the governor's race. Bennett was not renamed president until he announced in May that he would not run.[50]

Phillips remained quiet concerning the primary until July. Then he urged people to vote. He did not state a preference, but defended his administration and attacked his enemies. Kerr won the primary, becoming the Democratic nominee for governor, and Phillips was unhappy with the prospect of supporting him.

Finally, on October 8, 1942, Phillips bolted the Democratic Party by supporting Edward H. Moore instead of Josh Lee for United States Senator. Moore was an anti-New Deal Democrat running as a Republican. Phillips eventually also came out against Kerr, though he did not openly support the Republican candidate. The next day the leaders of the Democratic Party read Phillips out of the party. Phillips then began attacking both Kerr and Lee in radio speeches. Though Kerr became governor, Moore won the election for United States Senator.[51]

In January, 1943, Phillips, in his final speech to the legislature, gave a summary of his administration. He spoke informally because he disregarded his prepared speech that a newspaper had published. He mentioned the $5 million surplus the state had accumulated under his guidance and questioned the legislature about its intention of continuing his policy of economy. At Kerr's inauguration Phillips heard the new governor promise complete cooperation with the federal government, and by inference heard his own administration condemned.[52] Phillips, however, did not seem to care, declaring: "I feel better than two fellows ought to feel."[53]

After leaving office, Phillips continued to campaign against the New Deal. He refused to attend a New Deal banquet held in June, 1943. When denouncing the affair, Phillips said that the New Deal had destroyed free elections and individual initiative. He announced his complete break with the Democratic Party, and his new affiliation with the Republican Party on June 12, 1943. Once out of office, Phillips was accused of taking a bribe, while he was governor, to grant a parole to a prisoner in the Oklahoma Penitentiary at McAlester. Though the first trial ended in a hung jury, he was acquitted in the second trail. After this episode, he was no longer active in politics. He rejoined the Democratic Party in the late 1940s, and gave his written support to Frank P. Douglass, contender in the Democratic primary for governor in 1950. He returned to law after completing his service as governor, practicing in Okemah. He died of a heart attack on March 27, 1958, while waiting for a client at the post office in Okmulgee. He was buried in Hillcrest Cemetery in Weleetka, Oklahoma.[54]

When Phillips became governor, Oklahoma was in debt. Late payment of taxes was acceptable, as was overspending by the various state departments. The federal government was designing dam projects for the state, but Oklahoma was losing valuable property due to these dams. As soon as he was in office, Phillips began working with these issues. His answers were not always popular, for it meant economy and attacking the federal government. He wanted to place the state on a cash basis, so he encouraged reductions in appropriations and stepped-up collection of taxes.

The common school bloc believed it was hardest hit by the budget cuts of Phillips. He was not against education, but believed that local goverments should share more of the cost of education; many had become lax in their collection of taxes. When the school bloc tried to prevent passage of the balanced budget amendment, Phillips proved what a fierce combatant he could be. After winning the fight, he took away Superintendent Crable's patronage power; Phillips was not one to forgive and forget.

The battles of Phillips with the federal government occurred when the government grew dramatically in scope and size. He resented this interference with state sovereignty, and tried to reverse the development. He believed that Oklahomans should be allowed to control their natural resources without interference from the federal government. He would not follow the crowd in supporting New Deal spending which he believed the federal government could not afford and which he considered outside of its sphere of power. Both during his administration and after, he campaigned against the New Deal.

Whether on the state or national level, Phillips was consistent in his policies. He was elected on a platform of fiscal responsibility, and tried to keep this pledge during his administration. Despite a few differences, he was on friendly terms with the legislature. He maintained control over the legislature for the four years of his term because he carried out his campaign promises, which enabled the public to continue its support for him. When he left office, he could look back with satisfaction. Though he would no longer be in control, the state, by the balanced budget amendment, was mandated to continue his fiscal policies, and not follow the New Deal trend of over-spending.

ENDNOTES

1 *Daily Oklahoman* (Oklahoma City), February 9, 1940, p. 1, July 13, 1940, p. 3, July 14, 1940, p. 1; Leon C. Phillips Scrapbook, p. 15, Leon C. Phillips Collection, Western History Collections, University of Oklahoma, Norman, Oklahoma.

2 *Daily Oklahoman*, November 13, 1938, p. D-1, November 14, 1938, p. 14, November 15, 1938, p. 6.

3 *Ibid.*, November 15, 1938, p. 2-6, November 16, 1938, p. 12; *Who Was Who In America*, 4 vols. (Chicago: A. N. Marquis Company, 1960), Vol. III, p. 685.

4 *Daily Oklahoman*, November 16, 1938, p. 12, November 17, 1938, p. 12, November 18, 1938, p. 6; Robert Sobel and John Raimo, eds., *Biographical Directory of the Governors of the United States, 1789-1978*, 4 vols. (Westport, Connecticut: Meckler Books, 1978), Vol. III, p. 1249.

5 *Daily Oklahoman*, November 19, 1938, p. 6.

6 *Ibid.*, November 22, 1938, p. 20.

7 *Ibid.*, November 23, 1938, p. 11.

8 *Ibid.*, November 23, 1938, p. 11, November 25, 1938, p. 6.

9 *Ibid.*, November 27, 1938, p. A-7; U. S. Russell, "'Red' Phillips Puts Punch Into State Campaign," *Harlow's Weekly*, Vol. XLIX, No. 4 (January, 1938), pp. 7-8.

10 Russell, "'Red' Phillips Puts Punch Into State Campaign," *Harlow's Weekly*, Vol. XLIX, No. 4, p. 8

11 *Ibid.*, pp. 8-9.

12 *Ibid.*

13 *Ibid.*

14 *Ibid.*, p. 7.

15 "About Politics and Politicians," *Harlow's Weekly*, Vol. XLIX, No. 5 (January, 1938), p. 10, "About Politics and Politicians," *ibid.*, Vol. XLIX, No. 16 (April, 1938), p. 10, "About Politics and Politicians," *ibid.*, Vol. XLIX, No. 24 (June, 1938), p. 6; *Daily Oklahoman*, July 1, 1938, p. 1.

16 "About Politics and Politicians," *Harlow's Weekly*, Vol. XLIX, No. 15 (April, 1938), p. 12; *Daily Oklahoman*, July 1, 1938, p. 1, July 5, 1938, p. 1, July 11, 1938, p. 1, July 14, 1938, p. 1, July 17, 1938, p. 1.

17 *Daily Oklahoman*, August 13, 1938, p. 3, September 16, 1938, p. 11; Leon C. Phillips Scrapbook, p. 1, Leon C. Phillips Collection, Western History Collections, University of Oklahoma.

18 *Daily Oklahoman*, November 14, 1938, p. 1.

19 *Ibid.*, November 9, 1938, p. 1, November 15, 1938, p. 7, November 16, 1938, p. 1; *Okemah Daily Leader* (Okemah), November 8, 1938, p. 1.

20 *Daily Oklahoman*, January 9, 1939, p. 1, January 10, 1939, pp. 1-2, January 11, 1939, pp. 1-2; Victor E. Harlow, "Editorial," *Harlow's Weekly*, Vol. LI, No. 23 (January, 1939), p. 2; *Daily Oklahoman*, January 7, 1939, p. 1.

21 *Daily Oklahoman*, January 6, 1939, pp. 1-2, March 26, 1939, p. 10-A; U. S. Russell, "Beneath the Veneer of State Government," *Harlow's Weekly*, Vol. LI, No. 14 (January, 1939), p. 9; Oklahoma Senate, *Journal of the Senate, Seventeenth Legislature, Regular Session, 1939*, p. 110; Oklahoma House, *Journal of the House of Representatives, Seventeenth Legislature, Regular Session, 1939*, 2 vols. (Oklahoma City: Leader Press, 1939), Vol. I, pp. 205-208.

22 *Daily Oklahoman*, March 1, 1939, p. 1, February 16, 1939, p. 2.

[23] U. S. Russell, "Senate Surrenders Its Patronage at Phillips' Demand," *Harlow's Weekly*, Vol. LI, No. 13 (April, 1939), p. 14.

[24] *Daily Oklahoman*, March 1, 1939, p. 1, March 3, 1939, p. 1, February 16, 1939, p. 2; Oklahoma Senate, *Journal of the Senate, 1939*, p. 1052; Oklahoma House, *Journal of the House of Representatives, 1939*, Vol. I, p. 1328.

[25] *Daily Oklahoman*, January 5, 1939, p. 1, March 15, 1939, p. 6, March 16, 1939, p. 1, April 9, 1939, April 16, 1939, p. A-2; *Time Magazine*, Vol. XXXV, No. 4 (January 22, 1940), pp. 20-21.

[26] *Daily Oklahoman*, January 1, 1939, p. 1, January 5, 1939, p. 1, January 15, 1939, p. 1, January 17, 1939, p. 2, February 2, 1939, p. 1, February 3, 1939, p. 4; U. S. Russell, "Drastic Appropriations Cuts Have Legislature Worried," *Harlow's Weekly*, Vol. LI, No. 6 (February, 1939), p. 8; Oklahoma Senate, *Journal of the Senate, 1939*, p. 407; Oklahoma House, *Journal of the House of Representatives, 1939*, p. 749.

[27] *Daily Oklahoman*, February 5, 1939, p. A-1, February 9, 1939, pp. 1-2, February 11, 1939, p. 2, February 15, 1939, p. 9, February 21, 1939, p. 1, March 1, 1939, p. 1; Oklahoma House, *Journal of the House of Representatives, 1939*, pp. 947-975.

[28] *Daily Oklahoman*, March 1, 1939, p. 4, February 19, 1939, p. A-15, April 25, 1939, p. 1, April 28, 1939, p. 1.

[29] *Ibid.*, February 26, 1940, p. 1.

[30] *Ibid.*, February 28, 1940, p. 1, March 23, 1940, p. 3; Address of Governor Leon C. Phillips Broadcasted over KOMA and KTUL on March 19, 1940, Leon C. Phillips Collection, Western History Collections, University of Oklahoma.

[31] *Daily Oklahoman*, March 14, 1940, p. 1.

[32] *Ibid.*, March 15, 1940, p. 16.

[33] *Ibid.*, March 20, 1940, p. 1, March 22, 1940, p. 3, March 29, 1940, p. 5, February 4, 1941, pp. 1-2, December 2, 1941, p. 5.

[34] *Ibid.*, February 13, 1940, p. 1, March 10, 1940, p. 1, April 30, 1940, p. 9, February 25, 1941, p. 1, March 2, 1941, pp. A-10-12, December 5, 1941, p. 6; U.S. Russell, "Federal-State Clash over Red River Dam," *Harlow's Weekly*, Vol. LI, No. 3 (January, 1939), pp. 6-7.

[35] *Daily Oklahoman*, January 7, 1941, p. 1.

[36] *Ibid.*, January 5, 1941, p. 1; *New York Times* (New York, New York), October 19, 1941, Sec. II, p. 7.

[37] *Daily Oklahoman*, February 7, 1941, p. 1, February 8, 1941, p. 1, March 2, 1941, p. A-8.

[38] *Ibid.*, February 12, 1941, p. 1, February 23, 1941, p. 1, March 2, 1941, p. 1.

[39] *Ibid.*, March 12, 1941, p. 1.

[40] *Ibid.*, February 13, 1941, p. 1 March 21, 1941, p. 7, March 25, 1941, p. 1 April 16, 1941, p. 1.

[41] *Ibid.*, April 3, 1941, p. 2, May 17, 1941, p. 2; Oklahoma Senate, *Journal of the Senate, Eighteenth Legislature, Regular Session and First Extraordinary Session, 1941* (Oklahoma City: Leader Press, 1941), pp. 1284, 1786-1788, 1875; Oklahoma House, *Journal of the House of Representatives, Eighteenth Legislature, Regular Session, 1941*, 2 vols. (Oklahoma City: Leader Press, 1941), Vol. I, p. 2492, Vol. II, p. 3787.

[42] *Daily Oklahoman*, January 10, 1941, p. 1, May 1, 1941, p. 5, May 24, 1941, p. 1; Oklahoma Senate, *Journal of the Oklahoma Senate, 1941*, p. 1490; Oklahoma House, *Journal of the Oklahoma House of Representatives, 1941*, Vol. II, p. 3063.

[43] *Daily Oklahoman*, March 29, 1941, p. 1.

[44] *Ibid.*, March 22, 1941, p. 1, March 29, 1941, p. 1, May 8, 1941, p. 1.

[45] *Ibid.*, December 10, 1941, p. 7.

[46] *Ibid.*

[47] *Ibid.*, December 10, 1941, p. 16, December 12, 1941, p. 4, December 19, 1941, p. 1, January 27, 1942, p. 1.

[48] *Ibid.*, December 21, 1941, p. A-14, December 30, 1941, p. 11, January 29, 1942, p. 1.

[49] *Ibid.*, February 19, 1942, p. 5.

[50] *Ibid.*, January 11, 1942, p. A-6, January 18, 1942, p. A-2, February 24, 1942, p. 18,

March 15, 1942, p. A-8, April 14, 1942, p. 4, May 7, 1942, p. 1.

51 *Ibid.*, July 13, 1942, p. 1, October 9, 1942, p. 1, October 10, 1942, p. 1, November 1, 1942, p. A-12, November 4, 1942, p. 1.

52 *Ibid.*, January 12, 1943, p. 1; *Tulsa World* (Tulsa), January 6, 1943, pp. 1,4.

53 *Daily Oklahoman*, January 12, 1943, p. 1.

54 *Ibid.*, March 28, 1958, pp. 1-2; Leon C. Phillips to Phil Lowry, undated, file, "Republican Letter-Material," Frank P. Douglas to Leon C. Phillips, July 8, 1950, Leon C Phillips to Johnston Murray, April 25, 1950, file, "Correspondence Democratic-General," Box 8, Leon C. Phillips Collection, Western History Collections, University of Oklahoma; *Tulsa World*, June 13, 1943, Sec. 1, p. 1; Sobel and Raimo, eds., *Biographical Directory of the Governors of the United States, 1789-1978*, Vol. III, p. 1249.

Robert Samuel Kerr

Governor of Oklahoma, 1943-1947

By William P. Corbett

Robert Samuel Kerr

On May 22, 1943, Governor Robert Samuel Kerr traveled to Muskogee, Oklahoma, to survey damage caused by recent floods. Several days of torrential rains and high winds had ended abruptly the driest spring eastern Oklahomans had experienced in nineteen years. At first residents of the area welcomed the heavy showers, but as small streams overflowed their banks and as drainage ditches failed to carry away the runoff, a dangerous situation developed. The three great rivers of the region, the Arkansas, the Grand, and the Verdigris, normally shallow and listless, rose rapidly above flood level and caused widespread destruction. Before the rain ended and the flood subsided, Governor Kerr acted to relieve the plight of the residents of the stricken area.[1]

Accompanied by officials of the United States Army Corps of Engineers, Kerr interviewed victims of the disaster, surveyed damage to cropland, and made provisions for relief operations. Shocked and disturbed by the physical and psychological damage caused by the flood, he determined to find a permanent solution to the problem. The governor's reaction to the flood of 1943 mirrored his approach to other issues during his administration.

As chief executive of the state of Oklahoma, Kerr readily accepted responsibility and promoted the welfare of his constituents.[2]

Perhaps Kerr possessed a special sense of duty because he was the first native-born governor of the state. In February of 1894, William Samuel Kerr and his wife Margaret packed their possessions in a covered wagon and moved from Milford, Texas, to Pontotoc County, Chickasaw Nation, Indian Territory. They leased 160 acres of heavy timbered land southwest of the small town of Ada and began to farm. For several months they lived in a tent until Kerr completed a fourteen-foot-square log cabin. Robert, their second child and first son, was born in this cabin on September 11, 1896. Five years later the family moved closer to Ada where young Kerr attended the public schools and at the age of nine joined the Baptist Church.[3]

As Kerr grew to maturity, his father instilled in him principles and ideals that became important in later life. He believe a man's family came first, but once economic security had been accomplished a successful career in public services became a desirable achievement. He encouraged his teenage son to work hard and to set ambitious goals. A lifelong Democrat and teetotaler, William Samuel Kerr became a model for his son. At the age of fifteen, young Kerr picked 396 pounds of cotton, but his father expressed disappointment when he failed to pick 400 pounds. On another occasion, burglars stole the entire Sunday school collection of $7.50. As treasurer of the church group, the teenager felt responsible. He went to work at a nearby cement plant and received fifteen cents for each ten-hour day. The young man stayed at the factory until he made enough money to repay the church.[4]

In the autumn of 1909, Kerr entered East Central Oklahoma Normal College at Ada, and for the next several years his experiences included a collegiate career, military service, and a business venture. He attended classes at East Central for two years and then transferred to Oklahoma Baptist University at Shawnee. In 1915, Kerr enrolled for the fall term at the University of Oklahoma in Norman, but World War I interrupted his studies. He reported to Fort Logan H. Root, near

Little Rock, Arkansas, where he underwent training as an officer of artillery. Commissioned a second lieutenant, Kerr departed for France in the summer of 1918, but the war ended before his unit received orders to a combat zone. The following spring he returned home, negotiated a loan, and entered the produce business in Ada. This venture proved short lived and ended unhappily when fire consumed the young entrepreneur's warehouse.[5]

Heavily in debt, Kerr decided to pursue a career in law. He took a position in the office of John F. McKeel, a local judge, and began to prepare for the state bar examination. The apprentice attorney, moreover, did not completely immerse himself in the study of law. On Demember 5, 1919, he married Reba Shelton, whose brother was Kerr's partner in the produce business. Within three years Kerr passed the bar examination and opened a law office in Ada in partnership with two other attorneys. Aside from the responsibilities of his new career, he participated actively in civic affairs. He became a charter member of the local American Legion post, helped organize Battery F of the 160th Field Artillery, Oklahoma National Guard, and taught Sunday school at the First Baptist Church. As a result of his activities in the Baptist Church, Kerr gained recognition as an excellent speaker and often received invitations to deliver talks at other functions in the community. In February of 1924, however, the aspiring attorney suffered a personal tragedy when Reba Kerr and their firstborn child died in childbirth.[6]

The following year Kerr's personal and professional fortunes began to change. During the summer he made the acquaintance of a young, tall, blonde woman from Tulsa. Grayce Breene came to Ada to visit her sister and met the young attorney on a local tennis court. They began to see each other, and on their third date he announced his intention to marry her. The ceremony took place on December 26, 1925, and their marriage eventually produced four children: Robert, Jr.; Breene; Kay; and William.[7] Soon after the wedding, Kerr became the attorney for James L. Anderson, an oil drilling contractor and husband of Kerr's sister Mildred. The two men formed the Anderson-Kerr Drilling Company and invested in several wells in the oil fields at

Oklahoma City. As oil gushed from one well after another, the personal fortunes of the partners increased, and they invested more capital in the Oklahoma City oil basin. In 1936, Anderson retired, and Dean A. McGee, former chief geologist for the Phillips Petroleum Company, joined Kerr. The company grew rapidly and reached a net worth of more than $7 million in 1942. When McGee became executive vice-president in 1946, he joined Kerr to found Kerr-McGee Oil Industries, Incorporated. By 1959, the assets of Kerr-McGee totaled more than $200 million, and the personal fortune of Robert S. Kerr approximated $20.8 million.[8]

In 1932, Kerr had moved his family to Oklahoma City, and became active in the state's Democratic Party. He channeled most of his energy in the direction of raising funds for candidates. In 1934, he helped arrange financial support for Ernest W. Marland's successful gubernatorial campaign. Four years later, Kerr supervised most of the funding for the election of Leon C. Phillips as governor. In 1940, Kerr actively campaigned for the position of Democratic national committeeman for Oklahoma. Governor Phillips supported his candidacy, and officials of the party elected the properous oilman to the post. This exposure to national party politics, and his outspoken support of President Franklin D. Roosevelt at the Democratic National Convention in Chicago in 1940, made Kerr a public figure in Oklahoma and provided the opportunity for his particiption in the gubernatorial campaign in 1942.[9]

In December of 1941, the United States entered World War II, and Oklahomans, like others in the United States, focused their attention upon the emergencies created by the war. As the fighting unfolded through the first months of 1942, strife of another kind racked the Democratic Party in Oklahoma. Soon after his election, Governor Phillips had surprised many supporters and constituents when he announced his opposition to the New Deal. At the Democratic convention in Chicago he opposed Roosevelt's bid for a third term, but a portion of the state's delegation led by Kerr supported the president. After the national convention, the split within the delegation extended to the entire Democratic Party in Oklahoma, and Phillips and Kerr became bitter political enemies. Early in 1942, the oilman-turned-politician spoke out against the administration of Governor Phillips and, although not a declared candidate for the governorship, he began to talk like one. On April 13, 1942, before approximately 1,000 supporters at the junior high school in Ada, Kerr announced his candidacy and vehemently attacked Phillips.[10]

The campaign that followed was marked by a bitterly contested primary. Kerr wasted no time in declaring a platform that called for greater cooperation with the national government, a balanced budget for essential expenses only, and an overhaul of the Oklahoma Department of Education. These issues received little attention as the campaign became a contest between Kerr and Governor Phillips. Because the governor could not succeed himself, he actively supported Gomer Smith, a former congressman.[11] Yet Kerr continued to attack Phillips, particularly for his failure to accept the New Deal, which Kerr regarded as "regrettable and reprehensible."[12] Smith entered the fray to support his mentor. He charged that Kerr represented the state's petroleum interest and acted like a Republican disguised as a Democrat. Because of greater interest by the public in the progress of the war, an unusually small number of voters went to the polls on July 14, 1942, and gave Kerr a plurality of approximately 10,500 votes over Smith.[13]

The spirited nature of the gubernatorial contest continued until the general election in November. Early in October, Governor Phillips bolted the Democratic Party to support William J. Otjen, the Republican nominee for governor. This action further fueled the Kerr-Phillips conflict. The two factions virtually ignored Otjen as Phillips made statewide speeches on radio to urge the defeat of the Democratic contender, and Kerr accused the governor of fiscal irresponsibility. Despite the speeches, charges and counter charges, the electorate remained apathetic and less than 400,000 voters cast ballots on election day. Kerr received approximately 16,000 votes more than Otjen, but the Republican candidate contested the results. He filed a lawsuit with the Oklahoma Election Board to obtain a recount of the entire state. The election board dismissed the

On January 11, 1943, Kerr took the oath of office as governor of Oklahoma. Governor Kerr's election campaign brought vigorous opposition from outgoing Governor Leon C. Phillips, seated immediately behind Kerr (Western History Collections, University of Oklahoma).

petition, but Otjen took his case to the Oklahoma Supreme Court. The court found no justification for the suit and declared Kerr the winner.[14]

On January 11, 1943, the governor-elect took the oath of office and soon thereafter approached the Oklahoma Legislature with his program. The Democrats enjoyed a comfortable majority in the house of representatives and in the senate, and the new governor cultivated a close working relationship with the lawmakers. He preferred to meet in quiet conferences with the leaders of the legislature rather than resort to threats or use patronage to gain their support. As a result, the governor and the legislature cooperated on most major issues.[15]

Governor Kerr placed first priority on retirement of the state debt. Previous administrations had accumulated a total indebtedness of more than $36 million. Kerr proposed a plan of strict economy and requested legislators to permit the applicaion of surplus funds toward retirement of the debt. The governor curtailed expenditures for several executive departments through arbitrary cuts in the budget and by a reduction in the number of employees. He also refused the services of a personal bodyguard and reduced the size of the security force at the capitol. The legislature responded by passing a bill to create the Oklahoma School Bond Retirement Fund. This law provided for the transfer of surplus funds from the preceding fiscal year to purchase more than $5 million in bonds held by the Oklahoma School Land Department.[16]

The governor pressed for further fiscal restraint when he opposed a reduction in taxes. In the early 1940s many industries vital to the production of materials for war moved to Oklahoma. This rapid industrial growth provided the state with a measure of wartime prosperity. As a result, some Republican members of the house of representatives proposed repeal of the state income tax. Other legislators agitated for a reduction in the levy on auto licenses. Although the governor promised to institute no new taxes, he adamantly refused to support changes in the revenue laws unless the legislature provided alternative measures to replace any reduction of the state's income. Because Kerr implemented a program of "puritanic economy," the state debt was retired by 1945.[17]

Aside from fiscal matters, the governor supported amendments to Oklahoma's constitution. He opposed the unrestricted power of the governor to grant clemency to criminals, and he proposed that the legislature act upon an amendment to create a non-partisan Oklahoma Pardon and Parole Board. In February of 1943, the lawmakers presented the governor with legislation that provided for a five-member review board to examine all requests for clemency. The duties of the board's membership included the investigation of all applicants for commutation and recommendation to the governor by a majority vote of persons they believed qualified for clemency.[18]

Two other amendments affected several of Oklahoma's institutions of higher learning. Kerr wanted to remove the governing bodies of the state's agricultural colleges and of the University of Oklahoma from political domination and control. He proposed one amendment to establish a board of regents for the Oklahoma Agricultural and Mechanical College at Stillwater and for smaller tax-supported agricultural schools throughout the state. Members of the board, which included the president of the Oklahoma Board of Agriculture and eight others appointed by the governor, were to serve eight-year terms. For the University of Oklahoma, the governor asked the legislature to create a seven-member board of regents appointed by the governor for terms of seven years. Again lawmakers accommodated the governor and provided the necessary legislation. In July of 1944, voters approved both of these measures as well as the creation of the Oklahoma Pardon and Parole Board.[19]

The Oklahoma Democratic platform of 1942 committed Kerr to initiate changes in the state's primary election law. The Democrats planned to adopt a preferential primary to prevent the nomination of a candidate who received less than a majority of the vote. In 1925 a preferential primary law had passed the legislature, but the Oklahoma Supreme Court declared it unconstitutional. Four years later legislators enacted a law that provided for a runoff primary for nominees who did not receive a majority in the regular primary. This act was repealed in 1937. Kerr urged the adoption of a preferential primary system in order to eliminate the expense of a runoff primary. The lawmakers, however, reinstituted the runoff primary. This law was the last significant act of the legislature in 1943, and it adjourned at the end of April.[20]

Because of unique circumstances created by World War II, Governor Kerr called a special session of the Oklahoma Legislature on April 10, 1944. The legislators convened to make changes in absentee voting procedures. In order to expedite passage of the legislation, leaders of the house and senate submitted identical bills to their colleagues. Members of the house of representatives debated the issue for two days, and on April 13 a shouting match erupted that nearly boiled over into a fist fight. Creekmore Wallace, the Democratic whip, moved to vote final passage on the bill before the entire proposal had been read to the legislators. George E. Davison, Republican representative from Ellis County, challenged Wallace, and only the timely intervention of the sergeant-at-arms prevented an altercation. The tension subsided in subsequent meetings, and the bill passed. The act, which Governor Kerr promptly signed, provided for eligible Oklahomans on active duty in the armed forces outside of the state to use the federal short-form ballot in the general election of 1944. Perhaps this law increased the popularity of the Democrats, but so few sevicemen took advantage of it as to render no appreciable effect on the outcome of the election.[21]

When the regular session of the legislature assembled in January of 1945, military successes by the Allied nations assured victory over the Axis powers. As a result, the governor prepared a program for the postwar development of Oklahoma. Kerr reversed completely his ardent stance for economy in state government and outlined legislation that called for increased spending. After a perfunctory allusion to tax reduction, he called upon the lawmakers to vote increased funds for support of public schools, for construction of roads, for improvement of public health services, and for tax incentives for individuals and industries. These proposals necessitated the additional outlay of approximately $22.9 million a year for two years, and the program required new revenues of about $9 million annually. Astounded, several legislators condemned the governor's plans and vowed to fight any proposal to raise taxes. This action effectively challenged Kerr's control of the legislature. He continued, however, to rely on conferences and mediation to secure the cooperation of the legislators, and he spoke on statewide raido to obtain support of the public.[22]

Financial aid to the public schools comprised the largest amount of the new expenditures. The state's public education system had no permanent financial structure, and every two years during legislative sessions administrators and lobbyists went to the capital to secure funds for schools. The governor proposed a system of permanent funding, and he advocated adequate appropriations to upgrade the physical plants of schools, to increase the salaries of teachers, and to provide transportation for students. The legislators obliged the governor and allotted $15.6 million a year for two years. This appropriation almost doubled the amount made available for public education by the previous legislature.[23]

The legislature reacted favorably to other parts of the governor's program. In order to receive a larger share of federal matching funds for highways in Oklahoma, lawmakers enacted legislation that removed the disbursement of money for roads from county commissioners. The Oklahoma Highway Department became responsible for the allocation of funds, and the new law enabled the state to obtain an estimated $4 million more from the federal government than in previous years. Kerr also recommended a new public health program. His plan called for an assessment of the needs of the state and for funds to provide additional services. Once again the legislature passed laws that satisfied the governor and granted $1 million as an initial appropriation. Tax incentives, another of the governor's goals, received the attention of the legislature. A community property law enabled husbands and wives to save on their federal income taxes, and other statutes exempted some types of industrial machinery from use and sales levies.[24]

In order to balance the budget, Kerr asked for and received additional txes on several items. First, the legislature voted a two-cent per gallon increase for gasoline. This action produced new annual revenue of approximately $7 million. Second, the state's lawmakers raised the levy on automobile licenses, which they hoped would provide about $500,000 annually toward future expenses. Finally, the most controversial of the new revenue bills involved a large increase in the tax on beer. Many legislators feared revenge at the polls from their constituents if they supported the governor's proposal.[25] In reply to opponents of the beer bill, Governor Kerr, a teetotaler, remarked, "There is not a beer drinker who has to drink the slop if he doesn't want to pay the tax."[26] The bill passed, and during the last weeks of March, 1945, the state of Oklahoma began to collect an additional five dollars on each barrel of beer.[27]

Dr. Henry G. Bennett, the president of Oklahoma Agricultural and Mechanical College from 1928 to 1951, was indicted by a grand jury for conspiracy in a textbook scandal. Throughout the legal proceedings Governor Kerr became the subject of much criticism for openly supporting Bennett, his long-time personal friend (Special Collections, Oklahoma State University Library).

Although the governor's program and the new taxes attracted much attention, the investigation of a scandal from a previous administration caused a greater sensation. In December of 1942, Governor Leon C. Phillips filed a lawsuit on behalf of the people of Oklahoma that charged thirty-three individuals and textbook firms with defrauding the state of over $5.3 million in the selection of books for the public schools. One of the principals named in the petition was Dr. Henry G. Bennett, president of Oklahoma Agricultural and Mechanical College in Stillwater. Phillips alleged that Bennett, a close personal friend of Governor Kerr, and others had created the William H. Murray Education Foundation in 1934 for the purpose of extracting a 10 percent commission on the volume of business conducted by companies whose books the state adopted for use in the public schools. Although most of the members of the Murray Foundation were apparently innocent of any wrong-doing, the evidence against Bennett was particularly damaging. The petition specified arithmetic texts written by the college president had increased in price over a period of three years due to revisions. Upon examination, however, the new editions contained no actual changes from earlier volumes. Phillips also charged that Bennett failed to deposit royalties from sales of the books with the educational foundation as previously agreed.[28]

When Kerr became governor in January of 1943, he pressed for a legislative investigation. Leaders of the house of represenatives and of the senate appointed a joint committee to conduct the inquiry. Although Kerr approved of this action, the investigation progressed slowly. Advocates of the inquiry speculated the legislators procrastinated intentionally to protect colleagues from possible implication in the scandal. The governor met with the committee's membership and urged them to act but they continued to delay. The investigation did uncover payments made by publishers to Howard B. Drake, an official in Ernest W. Marland's administration, but the legislature adjourned before the committee produced any tangible results.[29]

Meanwhile, the lawsuit initiated by Phillips went to court. A county grand jury convened in Tulsa indicted Bennett on charges of conspiracy. During the subsequent trial, Kerr publicly supported his longtime friend. Enemies of the governor took advantage of the situation to attack him and made some progress in their attempt to damage his reputation. In December of 1943, Judge Bower Broaddus dismissed the case due to the expiration of the statute of limitations. Gomer Smith, attorney for the prosecution, appealed the verdict of Broaddus to the federal circuit court in Oklahoma City. He obtained permission for a new trial, and, in May of 1944, both sides presented their arguments. The court sustained the ruling handed down by Broaddus and dismissed the petition. Bennett continued as president of Oklahoma Agricultural and Mechanical College during the legal proceedings, and he retained that position until his death in 1951.[30]

The textbook scandal involved another high official of the state's public education system. Alvin L. Crable, the Oklahoma superintendant of public instruction, was named in the suit filed by Phillips, and he was indicted by the same grand jury that returned a true bill against Bennett. In 1937, Governor Marland appointed him superintendent to fill a vacancy created by the resignation of John S. Vaughn. The following year voters elected Crable to a full term and reelected him in 1942. Early in his career he became a close friend of Dr. Henry G. Bennett, which helped ensure his success in state school politics. The joint committee created during the regular session of the legislature in 1943 investigated charges of corruption lodged against Crable, but they found no basis for the accusations.[31]

When the Oklahoma Legislature convened in January of 1945, a house committee reopened the inquiry into the charges against Crable. Evidence presented during the investigation linked the superintendent with J. T. Daniel, speaker of the house during Marland's administration, and with Howard Drake. They allegedly received approximately $60,000 in bribes from publishers of textbooks. Within a month the committee returned six charges for impeachment against Crable, and the house opened debate on the issue. Although Governor Kerr released no public statements in support of the superintendent, he made known to the house of representatives his disapproval of the proceedings. The governor did not want lawmakers involved in a lengthy impeachment trial that could slow or prevent passage of his legislative program. For three days debate raged in the house chambers climaxed by a close vote against the recommendation to impeach Crable.[32]

Throughout his gubernatorial years, Kerr promoted a national reputation for Oklahoma by extension of himself. Aware of the state's potential for postwar expansion, he traveled across the country to boost Oklahoma as a site for new industry and as a center for agriculture. On one occasion the governor went to New York City to deliver a jug of sorghum molasses to a lady who wrote him to inquire about the syrup. Kerr also accepted invitations to speak to Democratic organizations in several states. In 1944, he appeared before numerous state conventions and heartily endorsed President Roosevelt's bid for a fourth term. Although criticized at home by some people for his frequent absences, Kerr paid his own expenses and continued to boost Oklahoma and the Democratic Party.[33]

In March of 1944, a special election for a vacant congressional seat thrust Oklahoma into national political news. In July of 1943, Jack A. Nichols, a Democrat, had resigned as representative from the Second Congressional District, which included the counties of Adair, Cherokee, Haskell, McIntosh, Muskogee, Okmulgee, Sequoyah, and Wagner. Recent gains by Republicans

While in New York City in 1943, Governor Kerr delivered a jug of sorghum molasses to Mr. and Mrs. Herman Brandner. Mrs. Brandner had written the governor to inquire about the syrup, and Kerr took advantage of the opportunity to promote this Oklahoma agricultural product (Oklahoma Publishing Company).

in general elections had reduced the Democratic majority in the United States House of Representatives to six votes, and Republican candidates had won eight of ten special congressional elections since 1942. The race in Oklahoma, moreover, became a battle between New Deal and anti-New Deal factions. Observers at the national level believed a win by anti-New Dealers would reflect a change in the national mood, which could effect the presidential campaign in the fall. The Republicans nominated E. O. Clark, who had lost the congressional election of 1942 to Nichols by only 385 votes. The Democrats selected William G. Stigler, a part-Choctaw attorney from Stigler, as their candidate.[34]

The individual identity of the participants lost all meaning as both parties recruited prominent politicians to help secure victory. Senator Edward H. Moore, an anti-New Deal Democrat from Oklahoma, spoke on behalf of Clark, and supporters of the Republican candidate brought in Senator W. Daniel Lee of

Texas. Lee, another Democratic opponent of the president, made several speeches against the policies of Roosevelt's administration. Meanwhile, Governor Kerr mobilized the regular Democratic organization in Oklahoma. Early in March he also contacted Robert E. Hannegan, national chairman of the Democratic Party. Hannegan agreed to provide as much assistance as possible. As a result, state party leaders invited Alben W. Barkley, senate majority leader, to take part in the campaign. Barkley arrived in Muskogee the day before the election. There Governor Kerr acted as master of ceremonies at a rally, and the senator spoke in defense of Roosevelt's administration and on behalf of Stigler. Apperently Kerr's tactics worked. Stigler won the election by approximately 3,700 votes, and the White House recognized the governor's role in the important victory.[35]

Oklahoma's governor continued to gain the confidence of Democratic Party leaders and, in June of 1944, they chose Kerr as the keynote speaker for the Democratic National Convention. Accompanied by several close friends and political associates, Kerr went to Chicago amid speculation that President Roosevelt considered him a potential nominee for the vice-presidency. The governor did not campaign actively for the position, and he became one of the first supporters of Harry S. Truman, the vice-presidential nominee. On July 19, 1944, Kerr delivered the keynote address before a capacity audience of 25,000 of the party faithful. He took issue with the platform and program proposed by the Republicans on domestic policy and foreign affairs. He labeled Thomas E. Dewey, the presidential nominee of the Republican Party, as inexperienced and praised the accomplishments of President Roosevelt. The speech generated such enthusiasm that on one occasion a massive demonstration in support of his remarks disrupted the proceedings. Kerr thoroughly enjoyed the convention, and the keynote speech promoted national recognition of Oklahoma and the governor.[36]

During the early years of his administration, Kerr obtained access to President Roosevelt. His subsequent rise within the ranks of the Democratic Party, and his ardent support of Roosevelt increased the governor's influence with the White

Governor Kerr in his hotel room as he prepared the keynote address for the Democratic National Convention in Chicago in 1944. This speech, delivered before a capacity audience and carried on nationwide radio, gained national recognition for Oklahoma and for Kerr (Western History Collections, University of Oklahoma Library).

House. Unique circumstances due to wartime conditions allowed the governor to intercede for constituents with the president. In 1943, he contacted Roosevelt to support the bid for Elmer Hale, president of the National Bank of McAlester, to retain his institution as the financial facility for the United States Naval Ammunition Depot at McAlester. President Roosevelt acknowledged Kerr's endorsement, and the National Bank of McAlester remained a depository of naval funds. The following year he appealed to Roosevelt to reduce the sentence of a young Oklahoman ordered dishonorably discharged as a result of a court martial. On another occasion he asked the commander-in-chief to influence the assignment of the only son of an Oklahoma family recently drafted into the army. Also, Kerr corresponded frequently with members of the president's staff and even exchanged Christmas greetings with the First Family.[37]

On April 12, 1945, President Roosevelt died at his residence at Warm Springs, Georgia. The following day Governor Kerr eulogized the late president in an emotional memorial address delivered to a joint session of the Oklahoma Legislature. The death of Roosevelt, however, did not appreciably diminish Kerr's influence with the White House. During the Democratic National Convention in 1944, he had gained the favor of Roosevelt's successor when he aided in the breakup of a coalition of favorite son candidates which enabled Truman to secure the vice-presidential nomination.[38]

During the immediate postwar era Kerr kept Oklahoma prominent in national political affairs. In May of 1946, he hosted the National Governors Conference at Oklahoma City. Prior to the convention, he had participated in other gubernatorial functions. In 1945, he served on the executive board of the national organization and presided at the annual meeting of the Southern Governors Conference planning committee. Later in 1946, he would chair the yearly session of the Southern Governors Conference at Miami Beach, Florida. Initially President Truman and thirty governors planned to attend the national conclave in Oklahoma City. A nationwide strike by railroad workers, however, forced the president to change his plans, and it kept eight of the governors at home. General Omar N. Bradley, director of the Veterans Administration, gave the main address at the three-day meeting, and the governors discussed such issues as conservation of natural resources and re-organization of the National Guard. Despite the problems caused by the railroad strike, the convention was judged one of the best National Governors Conferences, while Kerr was praised for his outgoing personality and organizational ability.[39]

In January of 1947, Kerr once again became a private citizen. On January 13 he accompanied his successor, Roy J. Turner, a millionaire oilman and rancher, to inaugural ceremonies at the capitol. Although he did not back Turner during the primary, he supported the cattleman in the runoff primary and in the general elections. Unlike his immediate predecessor, Kerr retired quietly from state politics relatively unscathed by criticism. He resumed his position as a principal officer in Kerr-McGee Oil Industries and prepared to run for the United States Senate.[40]

The senatorial contest of 1948 evolved into a bitter encounter much like the gubernatorial election six years earlier. Kerr traveled around the state in a private airplane and campaigned on the slogan "Land, Wood, and Water." He advocated the proper use and conservation of natural resources through irrigation, flood control, and hydroelectric projects to provide prosperity for Oklahoma. Gomer Smith, his chief opponent in the primary, wasted no time in exploiting Kerr's close relationship with President Truman. He asserted that the former governor supported the president's civil rights program and favored an end to segregation. In response, Kerr took the position that he would vote on such matters in accordance with the laws of the state of Oklahoma. In July of 1948, the oilman defeated Smith by more than 44,000 votes in the runoff primary. He then prepared to meet the Republican challenger Ross Rizley, a congressman from Guymon, who criticized his conservation program. At a speech before the Tulsa Chamber of Commerce, he altered Kerr's compaign slogan to "Land, Wood, Wind, and Water" and credited the third element to the Democratic contender. Kerr, nevertheless, dominated the general election and defeated the Republican by more than 170,000 votes. Thus Kerr became the first former governor from his state elected to the United States Senate, and Oklahomans reelected him in 1954 and again in 1960.[41]

Soon after Kerr arrived in Washington, D. C., he began to work for flood control and river navigation projects. The need to harness the three great rivers of eastern Oklahoma, the Arkansas, the Grand, and the Verdigris, had been impressed upon him by the flood of 1943 and by subsequent flooding disasters that had occurred during his gubernatorial years. The idea of such a vast program, however, originated years before

Governor Kerr entering the White House to meet with President Harry S. Truman to discuss development of the Arkansas River. Kerr won support from Truman to secure passage of legislation that created the Arkansas River Project (Western History Collections, University of Oklahoma).

Kerr became a senator. As early as 1923, the Oklahoma City Chamber of Commerce established a flood control committee to promote legislation for development of the region's rivers. They obtained state legislation to create a flood control commission for Oklahoma and to finance a survey of troublesome rivers. Ernest E. Blake, an attorney from Oklahoma City, served as spokesman for this group. In November of 1927, he appeared before the United States House of Representatives Committee on Flood Control, and testimony by Blake and others spurred the committeemen into action. The following year Congress enacted legislation that authorized the United States Army Corps of Engineers to prepare a flood control plan for the Mississippi River Valley system, which included the Arkansas River basin. Subsequent statutes provided funds for the construction of reservoirs on many of the tributary waterways. The Pensacola Dam, located on the Grand River near Disney, Oklahoma, was among the first of these projects.[42]

When Kerr became governor, he pressed for futher federal involvement. In 1943 he joined Ben T. Laney, the governor of Arkansas, to promote development of the Arkansas River. They authorized the Arkansas-Oklahoma Interstate Water Resources Committee comprised of three members from Arkansas and of Newton T. Graham, Donald O. McBride, and T. Elmer Harbour from Oklahoma. This organization served a twofold purpose. First, it focused upon mobilizing the support of the congressional delegations from the two states. Second, it prepared an indepth publication based upon studies compiled by the United States Army Corps of Engineers that provided a plausible plan for flood control, irrigation, hydroelectric, and navigation projects on the Arkansas River and its tributaries. Also, members of the committee, led by Graham, a banker from Tulsa, originated the strategy and acted as a "brain trust" for congressional hearings.[43]

As governor, Kerr promoted the work of the interstate commission. In August of 1944, he prevailed upon President Roosevelt to support the Arkansas River Project. But Roosevelt reacted indifferently as he placed war priorities ahead of long-range internal improvements. Kerr acheived greater success, however, when he approached President Truman, who expressed interest in the development of the waterway and responded favorably.[44] The chief executive informed Kerr: "I hope we will be able to get something done on the Arkansas River Project."[45] In July of 1946, the carefully orchestrated activities of the joint committee and the petitions of Governor Kerr came to fruition when Congress authorized $55 million for multipurpose development of the Arkansas River and its tributaries in the states of Arkansas and Oklahoma.[46]

In the senate Kerr worked vigorously to secure completion of the waterways program. One of his major goals was to obtain permanent appropriations for the Arkansas River Navigation Project, a major part of the Arkansas River Project. He became interested in the idea of an all-water route from the mouth of the Arkansas to Catoosa, Oklahoma, near Tulsa, through the efforts of Newton T. Graham and Donald O. McBride. Graham had promoted the project for many years as a means of reducing high overland freight rates for heavy equipment necessary to the oil industry. Through the mutual acquaintance fo McBride, a professional engineer, Graham gained Kerr's confidence. At first the senator from Oklahoma faced much criticism, and the absence of support from the administration of President Dwight D. Eisenhower provided many obstacles. Yet, Kerr persevered. In 1956, as a member of the Senate Appropriations Sub-committee and backed by the congressional delegations from Arkansas and Oklahoma, he secured funds that insured the preservation of the navigation project.[47]

Kerr also held other key positions in the senate. He chaired the Senate Rivers and Harbors Committee and served as the senior Democrat on the Senate Public Works Committee. These positions and his adamant support of the Arkansas River Navigation Project gained for him among critics a reputation as a pork barrel legislator. Hardly inconspicuous at six-feet-three-inches tall and more than two hundred pounds, he brimmed with confidence and readily admitted pride in his ability to obtain money for public works in Oklahoma. Eventually, Kerr emerged as a leader in the senate. His opposition to President John F. Kennedy's legislation to create Medicare helped to insure its defeat, but as chairman of the Senate Aeronautics and

Space Sciences Committee he managed a satellite communications bill supported by the administration through a determined filibuster. As a result of this action, Senator Paul H. Douglas, a Democrat from Illinois, dubbed Kerr the uncrowned king of the senate.[48]

On New Year's Day of 1963, the long career of public service rendered by Kerr ended. More than two weeks earlier he was admitted to a hospital in Washington, D.C., with what initially was believed to be an upper respiratory infection. For several months prior to hospitalization Kerr had complained of sporadic chest pains. On December 18 he suffered a severe heart attack, but attending doctors expected him to make a full recovery. As he sat in bed on the morning of January 1, he recounted to a nurse and to Dr. James L. Keating his first experience in New York City. He stopped suddenly in mid-sentence and fell back on the bed. He died instantly of a massive heart attack.[49]

Kerr's death shocked Oklahomans, and they prepared an elaborate funeral. A military aircraft assigned to the presidential fleet conveyed the remains to Tinker Air Force Base, near Oklahoma City. On January 3, the body laid in state in the rotunda of the state capitol where mourners filed by the casket flanked by a soldier and a state trooper. The following day dignitaries arrived in Oklahoma City for the funeral. President John F. Kennedy, Vice-President Lyndon B. Johnson and his wife, and congressional colleagues of the late senator numbered among the most prominent who attended the service at the Rose Hill Mausoleum. In February of 1963, the Oklahoma Legislature passed a joint resolution that declared the birthplace of Kerr a state memorial. Ten months later the body was removed from the mausoleum and was transported to the original family homestead two miles southeast of Ada. There, atop a hill that provides a panorama of Pecan Valley and of the restored log cabin of his birth, Kerr's remains were entombed in a large but not elaborate stone vault.[50]

As governor of Oklahoma, Kerr revealed the characteristics of a strong and determined leader. Through conferences and conciliatory gestures he secured the cooperation of the Oklahoma Legislature, and thus obtained passage of programs that served a specific and positive purpose. Early in his administration Kerr enforced a policy of strict fiscal restraint, which within two years retired the state's debt. He introduced reform measures intended to remove the boards of regents of the major state institutions of higher learning from political control, and he reduced the unbridled power of the governor to grant clemency with the creation of the Oklahoma Pardon and Parole Board.

During the last years of his administration, when Oklahoma emerged from its financial doldrums, Kerr reversed the penny-pinching policies implemented earlier. He took advantage of revenues newly created by wartime prosperity to increase funds for schools, highways, and public health services. Yet, he resisted attempts by legislators to reduce taxes, and he maintained a balanced budget. He also recognized Oklahoma's potential for postwar expansion and supported legislation to encourage economic development within the state.

An astute politician, Kerr tirelessly promoted both his native state and his own career. As an ardent Democrat and faithful supporter of President Roosevelt, Kerr became well-known outside Oklahoma as he traveled around the country speaking at functions of the Democratic Party. The prominence of the state and of the governor in national affairs increased as attention focused on the special congressional election of 1944, and Kerr enhanced this nationwide recognition through his keynote address at the Democratic National Convention of 1944. Only the textbook scandal marred the governor's reputation, but his sole connection with it was to defend an implicated longtime personal friend. Kerr, nevertheless, continued to promote Oklahoma by sponsoring development of the Arkansas River. The enactment of federal legislation that created the Arkansas River Project opened new economic opportunities for the state and provided the basis for Kerr's subsequent career in national politics.

Cooperation, sound management, and progress characterized the administration of Kerr. He supplied the state with a firm financial plan, he worked with the Oklahoma Legislature to initiate new programs, and he sponsored long-range projects important for future development. Throughout his four years as governor, Kerr readily accepted responsibilities and promoted the welfare of his constituents.

ENDNOTES

1 *Tulsa Tribune* (Tulsa), May 22, 1943, p. 1, May 6, 1943, p. 1, May 8, 1943, p. 1, May 10, 1943, p. 1, May 11, 1943, p. 1, May 17, 1943, p. 1, May 19, 1943, p. 1, May 21, 1943, p. 1.

2 Robert S. Kerr, *Land, Wood, and Water* (New York: Fleet Publishing Corporation, 1960), pp. 159, 165-167.

3 Laura M. Messenbaugh, "William Samuel Kerr," *The Chronicles of Oklahoma*, Vol. XIX, No. 3 (September, 1941), pp. 250-251; *Daily Oklahoman* (Oklahoma City), July 22, 1942, p. 1; J. T. Salter, ed., *Public Men In and Out of Office* (Chapel Hill: University of North Carolina Press, 1946), pp. 424-425; *Daily Oklahoman*, July 24, 1942, p. 18.

4 *Daily Oklahoman*, July 22, 1942, pp. 1, 3, July 24, 1942, p. 18.

5 Gaston Litton, *A History of Oklahoma at the Golden Anniversary of Statehood*, 4 vols. (New York: Lewis Historical Publishing Company, 1957), Vol. I, p. 598; Salter, *Public Men In and Out of Office*, p. 425.

6 J. David Cox, "Robert S. Kerr and the Arkansas River Navigation Project: A Study in Legislature Leadership" (Doctor of Philosophy Dissertation, Norman: University of Oklahoma, 1972), p. 16; Jon H. Nabors, "Robert S. Kerr, A Baptist Layman: A Study of the Impact of Religion and Politics on the Life of an Oklahoma Leader" (Master of Arts Thesis, Norman: University of Oklahoma, 1964), pp. 13-14.

7 Salter, *Public Men In and Out of Office*, pp. 426-427; Nabors, "Robert S. Kerr, A Baptist Layman," pp. 15, 16.

8 Nabors, "Robert S. Kerr, A Baptist Layman," p. 17; David Seligman, "Senator Bob Kerr: The Oklahoma Gusher," *Fortune*, Vol. VIX, No. 3 (March, 1959), pp. 136, 182, 184; *Daily Oklahoman*, January 2, 1963, p. 6, March 31, 1964, p. 1.

9 Salter, *Public Men In and Out of Office*, pp. 426, 427.

10 *Ibid.*, p. 426; *Daily Oklahoman*, February 19, 1942, p. 5, February 22, 1942, Section A, p. 6, April 14, 1942, p. 4.

11 *Daily Oklahoman*, July 7, 1942, p. 2.

12 *Ibid.*

13 *Ibid.*, July 14, 1942, p. 1; Oklahoma Election Board, *Directory of the State of Oklahoma, 1943* (Guthrie: Co-operative Publishing Company, 1943), p. 19.

14 *Daily Oklahoman*, October 10, 1942, p. 4, November 4, 1942, p. 10, October 11, 1942, Section A, p. 6, November 1, 1942, pp. 1, 12; Oklahoma Election Board, *Directory of the State of Oklahoma, 1943*, p. 18; *Daily Oklahoman*, November 3, 1942, p. 1, November 17, 1942, p. 1; *Oklahoma Reports: Cases Determined by the Supreme Court of the State of Oklahoma* (Tulsa: Mid-West Publishing Company, 1943), Vol. 191 A, pp. 628-644.

15 *Daily Oklahoman*, November 15, 1942, Section A, p. 10, January 11, 1943, p. 1; Salter, *Public Men In and Out of Office*, p. 421.

16 *Daily Oklahoman*, January 2, 1944, Section A, p. 8; Oklahoma House, *Journal of the House of Representatives, Nineteenth Legislature, 1943*, 2 vols. (Oklahoma City: Leader Press, 1943), Vol. I, p. 100; *Daily Oklahoman*, February 7, 1943, Section A, p. 2, January 24, 1943, p. 1, January 6, 1943, p. 1; Oklahoma Legislature, *Official Session Laws, 1943* (Guthrie: Co-operative Publishing Company, 1943), pp. 139-142.

17 *Daily Oklahoman*, February 6, 1943, pp. 1, 2, January 11, 1945, p. 2, January 1, 1943, p. 1, February 3, 1943, p. 1; Oklahoma House, *Journal of the House of Representatives, 1943*, Vol. I, p. 97; Litton, *A History of Oklahoma at the Golden Anniversary of Statehood*, Vol. I, p. 598.

[18] Oklahoma House, *Journal of the House of Representatives, 1943*, Vol. I, p. 108; Oklahoma Legislature, *Official Session Laws, 1943*, pp. 341, 342.

[19] Oklahoma House, *Journal of the House of Representatives, 1943*, Vol. I, p. 114; Oklahoma Legislature, *Official Session Laws, 1943*, pp. 340, 349, 350; *Daily Oklahoman*, July 12, 1944, p. 1.

[20] Oklahoma House, *Journal of the House of Representatives, 1943*, Vol. I, pp. 105, 106; *Daily Oklahoman*, January 2, 1943, p. 1; Oklahoma Legislature, *Official Session Laws, 1943*, p. 90.

[21] *Daily Oklahoman*, April 10, 1944, p. 2, April 13, 1944, pp. 1, 2; Oklahoma Legislature, *Official Session Laws, 1944* (Guthrie: Co-operative Publishing Company, 1944), pp. 3-11; Litton, *A History of Oklahoma at the Golden Anniversary of Statehood*, Vol I, pp. 599, 600.

[22] *Daily Oklahoman*, January 3, 1945, p.1, March 27, 1945, p. 1, February 6, 1945, p. 1, January 28, 1945, Section A, p. 2, February 10, 1945, p. 3, April 1, 1945, Section A, p. 10.

[23] Oklahoma House, *Journal of the House of Representatives, Twentieth Legislature, Regular Session, 1945*, 2 vols. (Oklahoma City: Leader Press, 1945), Vol. I, pp. 42-44; *Daily Oklahoman*, February 9, 1945, p. 1; Oklahoma Legislature, *Official Session Laws, 1943*, p. 295; Oklahoma Legislature, *Official Session Laws, 1945* (Guthrie: Co-operative Publishing Company, 1945), p. 463.

[24] *Daily Oklahoman*, January 17, 1945, p. 4, April 25, 1945, p. 12, April 11, 1945, p. 1; Oklahoma Legislature, *Official Session Laws, 1945*, pp. 118-122, 224-235, 276.

[25] *Daily Oklahoman*, April 12, 1945, pp. 1, 2, April 13, 1945, p. 15; Oklahoma Legislature, *Official Session Laws, 1945*, pp. 145-146, 267.

[26] *Daily Oklahoman*, March 2, 1945, p. 1.

[27] Oklahoma Legislature, *Official Session Laws, 1945*, p. 489; *Daily Oklahoman*, March 21, 1945, p. 1.

[28] *Daily Oklahoman*, January 1, 1943, p. 1.

[29] Salter, *Public Men In and Out of Office*, p. 424; *Daily Oklahoman*, January 18, 1943, p. 1, February 12, 1943, p. 1, March 25, 1943, p. 2.

[30] *Muskogee Times-Democrat* (Muskogee), January 3, 1944, p. 1; *Daily Oklahoman*, January 12, 1947, Section D, p. 1, May 21, 1944, Section A, p. 8; *Tulsa Tribune*, May 7, 1943, p. 18; *Who Was Who in America*, 7 vols. (Chicago; A. N. Marquis Company, 1960), Vol. VII, p. 67.

[31] *Muskogee Times-Democrat*, January 3, 1944, p. 1; *Daily Oklahoman*, February 12, 1945, p. 1, February 9, 1945, p. 4; Lyle H. Boren and Dale Boren, *Who Is Who in Oklahoma* (Guthrie: Co-operative Publishing Company, 1935), p. 113.

[32] *Daily Oklahoman*, February 3, 1945, p. 1, January 2, 1944, p. A-8, February 9, 1945, pp. 1, 4, February 15, 1945, p. 1, February 16, 1945, p. 1.

[33] Litton, *A History of Oklahoma at the Golden Anniversary of Statehood*, Vol. I, p. 601; *Daily Oklahoman* January 12, 1947, Section D, p. 1.

[34] *New York Times* (New York, New York) March 28, 1944, pp. 1, 13, March 29, 1944, p. 1; *Daily Oklahoman*, March 30, 1944, p. 1, March 29, 1944, pp. 1, 2.

[35] *Daily Oklahoman*, March 20, 1944, p. A-2, March 29, 1944, p. 1, March 28, 1944, pp. 1, 2; *Muskogee Times-Democrat*, March 21, 1944, p. 1; Eugene Casey to Robert S. Kerr, March 29, 1944, Robert S. Kerr Collection, Western History Collections, University of Oklahoma, Norman, Oklahoma; Oklahoma Election Board, *Directory of the State of Oklahoma, 1945* (Guthrie: Co-operative Publishing Company, 1945), p. 18; Eugene Casey to Robert S. Kerr, March 29, 1944, Kerr Collection.

[36] *New York Times*, June 16, 1944, p. 32; *Daily Oklahoman*, July 16, 1944, p. 1, July 20, 1944, p. 1; Salter, *Public Men In and Out of Office*, p. 417; Robert S. Kerr, "Aims and Purposes," *Vital Speeches of the Day*, Vol. X, No. 20 (August 1, 1944), pp. 611-616; Robert S. Kerr to James M. Barnes, August 16, 1944, Kerr Collection.

[37] Litton, *A History of Oklahoma at the Golden Anniversary of Statehood*, Vol. I, p. 606; Robert S. Kerr to Franklin D. Roosevelt, December 6, 1943, Roosevelt to Kerr, December 17, 1943, telegram from Kerr to Roosevelt, May 18, 1944, Kerr to Roosevelt, August 7, 1944, Kerr to James M. Barnes, February 3, 1944, February 10, 1944, February 11, 1944, Roosevelt to Kerr, December 29, 1943, Kerr Collection.

38 *Daily Oklahoman,* April 13, 1945, p. 1, January 12, 1947, Section D, p. 1; Oklahoma House, *Journal of the House of Representatives, 1945,* Vol. II, pp. 2431-2435.

39 *Thirty-Eighth Annual Meeting: Governors Conference* (n.p.: n.p., 1945), p. 1, Kerr Collection; *Proceedings of the Governors Conference, 1945* (Chicago: The Governors Conference, 1945), p. v, Kerr Collection; *Proceedings of the Southwards Planning Committee of the Southern Governors Conference* (n.p., 1947), p. 1, Kerr Collection; *New York Times,* May 22, 1946, p. 19, May 27, 1946, p. 2, May 28, 1946, p. 44, May 29, 1946, p. 17; Frank Bane to Robert S. Kerr, June 3, 1946, Kerr Collection.

40 *Daily Oklahoman,* January 12, 1947, Section D, p. 1; Marquis W. Childs, "The Big Boom From Oklahoma," *Saturday Evening Post,* Vol. CCXXI, No. 1 (April 9, 1949), p. 119.

41 Childs, "The Big Boom From Oklahoma," *Saturday Evening Post,* Vol. CCXXI, p. 119; Kerr, *Land, Wood, and Water,* p. 168; Oklahoma Election Board, *Directory of the State of Oklahoma, 1959* (Guthrie: Co-operative Publishing Company, 1959) p. 40; Oklahoma Election Board, *Directory of the State of Oklahoma, 1949* (Guthrie: Co-operative Publishing Company, 1949), p. 22; Claude R. Thorpe, "Robert S. Kerr's 1948 Senatorial Campaign" (Master of Arts Thesis, Norman: University of Oklahoma, 1967), p. 71; Oklahoma Election Board, *Directory of the State of Oklahoma, 1961* (Guthrie: Co-operative Publishing Company, 1961) p. 28.

42 *Daily Oklahoman,* April 12, 1944, p. 1, April 15, 1945, p. 1; Minutes of the State Flood Control Legislation Committee, November 27, 1923, undated, unsigned memo, p. 1, Open Letter to Members of Oklahoma City Chamber of Commerce, November 23, 1929, Kerr-McBride Papers, Special Collections, Oklahoma State University Library, Stillwater, Oklahoma; Kerr, *Land, Wood, and Water,* pp. 94, 97, 98; "An Act for the Control of Floods on the Mississippi River and Its Tributaries," *Statutes at Large of the United States* (Washington: Government Printing Office, 1929), Vol. XLV, Part 1, pp. 534-539; "An Act Authorizing the Construction of Public Works on Rivers and Harbors for Flood Control," *Statutes at Large of the United States* (Washington: Government Printing Office, 1938), Vol. LII, pp. 1215-1226; United States House of Representatives, *Report 2353,* 75th Congress, 3rd sess., p. 20.

43 Kerr, *Land, Wood, and Water,* pp. 180, 181; *The States of Arkansas and Oklahoma Present Additional Benefits on the Prepared Comprehensive Improvement of the Arkansas River Basin* (n.p.: n.p, n.d.), pp. 6, 7, Kerr-McBride Papers; Thomas L. Reynolds, "Senator Robert S. Kerr and the Arkansas River Project" (Master of Arts Thesis, Stillwater: Oklahoma State University, 1964), p. 35.

44 Robert S. Kerr to Franklin D. Roosevelt, August 7, 1944, Roosevelt to Kerr, August 23, 1944, Kerr to Harry S. Truman, August 25, 1945, Kerr to Truman, May 14, 1946, Kerr Collection.

45 Harry S. Truman to Robert S. Kerr, May 18, 1946, *ibid.*

46 "An Act Authorizing the Construction, Repair, and Preservation of Certain Public Works on Rivers and Harbors," *Statutes at Large of the United States* (Washington: Government Printing Office, 1946), Vol. LX, Part 1, pp. 634-641.

47 Kerr, *Land, Wood, and Water,* pp. 174-177, 182.

48 *Daily Oklahoman,* January 2, 1963, pp. 2, 6; Seligman, "Senator Bob Kerr: The Oklahoma Gusher," *Fortune,* Vol. LIX, p. 137.

49 *Daily Oklahoman,* January 2, 1963, pp. 1, 2.

50 *Ibid.,* p. 1, January 3, 1963, p. 1, January 4, 1963, p. 1, January 5, 1963, p. 1, February 15, 1963, p. 12; December 14, 1963, p. 3; Oklahoma Legislature, *Oklahoma Session Laws, 1963* (St. Paul: West Publishing Company, 1963), p. 745.

Roy Joseph Turner

Governor of Oklahoma, 1947-1951

By Courtney Ann Vaughn-Roberson

Roy Joseph Turner

"I changed my party in 1946 so I could vote for Roy Turner in the Democratic primary," said Glen Vaughn, an old Oklahoma cattleman friend of Turner.[1] While Turner was not without political foes, his popularity with many Oklahomans was aptly described by this statement. His personality and programs offered an excellent combination of many types of political philosophies. In contrast to one of his opponents in the gubernatorial primary, H. C. Jones of Oklahoma City, Oklahoma, Turner was not an ardent New Dealer. On the contrary, he was a self-made man who earned a fortune in the oil and cattle businesses.

Turner supported the business sector of Oklahoma during his administration by encouraging industrial development through a decrease in income taxes. He never seemed to forget the young boy that he once was—the son of a Kendrick, Oklahoma, homesteader and livery stable owner. As a private citizen and as governor, Turner hosted an annual livestock exhibition and judging contest for 4-H Club and Future Farmers of America boys and girls, and he labored for and won legislation to provide farm-to-market roads and better organized rural school districts. But most of all, Turner never forgot his friends. "Even after Roy was governor, and I was still poor, I called him one day at his ranch," explained Vaughn. "A friend of mine wanted to see his 10,000 acre Hereford Heaven. Well, we ended up spending the day with him."[2]

The road from Turner's birthplace near Kendrick, Oklahoma, to the governor's office is a story of drive and struggle. Turner, the Horatio Alger of Lincoln County, was born on November 6, 1894, to Reason and Etta Louise Turner. He lived with them until he quit high school and moved to Oklahoma City, where he received his second and last bit of formal education from Hill's Business University. Eager to employ his skills, he was soon hired as a bookkeeper for Morris Packing Company in Oklahoma City, where he worked from 1911 to 1915. He displayed additional talents as a salesman for Goodyear Tire and Rubber Company in Oklahoma City, until he enlisted as a private in the Fifty-sixth Infantry Regiment, Seventh Division of the United States Army, during World War I.[3]

Although Turner's military service interrupted his career in the business world, he soon returned to yet another aspect of buying and selling, real estate. Land speculation, primarily in Oklahoma, Florida, and Texas, would eventually launch him into a lucrative future. While he was working in a clothing store in Florida, Turner met Forrest E. Harper, a man who would be one of the most important people in Turner's life. They struck up a friendship and a business partnership, but the Florida economic boom collapsed in the late 1920s, taking Turner and Harper with it.[4]

The team returned to Oklahoma, with barely enough money to eat. They lived in boarding houses in Oklahoma City, which accepted their rent money whenever they could afford to pay. Frank Clark, another generous benefactor to their cause, furnished them with an automobile and gasoline on credit. They bought and sold oil-rich land while they worked and hoped for financial opportunity to open for them. One day in the early 1930s it came. The Phillips Petroleum Company of Bartlesville, Oklahoma, offered to purchase some of their property for

$750,000. Instead of taking their shares and living extravagantly for a time, Harper and Turner retained royalties on the newly purchased property.[5]

In addition to the Harper-Turner investments in oil, they began in 1933 to build the famous Turner Hereford Heaven Ranch near Sulphur, Oklahoma. Harper wanted to raise commercial cattle, but Turner chose to breed his well-known purebred Hereford cattle. For this reason, four years after the ranch was purchased, Harper sold out to Turner, who in future years took an active part in the American Hereford Association; he served on its board of directors and as president three times between 1939 and 1945. The two men remained partners in the oil business until 1955, when Turner sold his interests to Harper.[6]

Romance as well as good fortune did not desert Turner, but he learned that marriage, like business, required work. His first marriage was short and produced no children. Fate reacquainted Turner in the 1930s with a woman, Jessica E. Grimm, whom he had once held on his lap when she was a child. Turner's father had died and his widow married Jessica's uncle. Although Turner was twenty years her senior, their affection eventully grew, and they were married in 1937. Later they increased their family to four by adopting twins, a boy they called Roy W. and a girl named Betty.[7]

Still newly married and already equipped with children, Turner unknowingly began his political career in 1939 when he was elected to the Oklahoma City School Board. He served well for seven years, making a name for himself as an honest man and as an interested community worker. In addition to school board experience, Turner spent much of his time between 1944 and 1946 at the Oklahoma Capitol making friends and entertaining legislators. Almost everyone around the capitol knew him by name. Encouraged by some of his ranching associates, he became a candidate for governor of Oklahoma in 1946.[8]

A diverse group of candidates challenged Turner in a hard fought and often bitter race to determine who would become the Democratic nominee. The three who offered Turner the most competition were William O. Coe, an Oklahoma City attorney and a World War II veteran; H. C. Jones, a former United States Internal Revenue collector for Oklahoma; and Dixie Gilmer, a Tulsa, Oklahoma, attorney. Although newspaper articles continually headlined Jones and Turner as the leading contenders, Gilmer would take second place and challenge Turner in the runoff primary late in July.

Throughout the campaign and during his term as governor, Turner proposed a program which would be called his "eleven points." It included an Oklahoma Highway Commisson reorganization plan, the creation of a much needed turnpike between Tulsa and Oklahoma City, and continued construction of farm-to-market roads. In striving for greater efficiency in other governmental agencies, he proposed reorganization of the Oklahoma Tax Commission and school board districts. Turner's plan included oftentimes forgotten people, because he pushed for improvements of veterans' programs, allotments of fifty dollars monthly for the aged, and benefits to state facilities such as mental hospitals. The growth of industry and agriculture was imperative to the funding of Turner's program, for he had pledged to decrease income taxes.[9]

Jones blasted Turner's schemes, especially the proposal for the reorganization of the state highway commission, which called for the gubernatorial appointment of eight new members. This gave too much power to the governor, who would appoint the new members, Jones complained. Jones, in keeping with his liberal views, promised to complete the road building policies of the present governor, Robert S. Kerr. Jones hammered also at some of Turner's advocates who opposed the graduated income tax concept. Turner fought back by branding Jones as the machine or administrative candidate. Paradoxically, Gilmer, an anti-New Deal advocate, accused both Turner and Jones of representing the Democratic machine in Oklahoma, the leaders of which he identified as Kerr, Dr. Henry G. Bennett, the president of Oklahoma Agricultural and Mechanical College, and Alvin L. Crable, the state superintendent of public instruction. In an attempt to secure the confidence of the voters, each man claimed to be the foe of autocrats.[10]

The primary, held on July 2, 1946, produced three top runners. Jones tallied 79,237 votes, Gilmer mustered 84,783, and Turner rallied with 138,348. When Turner was interviewed at his home shortly after realizing he had received the most votes, he was not sure if there would be a runoff primary. Little did he know that he would be involved with Gilmer in one of the most bitter political struggles in Oklahoma's history. Many of Jones's followers, significantly the labor and farm voters, gave their support to Turner, while Gilmer began a smear campaign which gained him some support.[11]

Gilmer flung vehement charges at Turner, centering his campaign promises around "cleaning out the capitol." Once again the familiar accusation that Turner was part of a Democratic machine characterized the Gilmer platform. Lunging also at Bennett, Gilmer promised that if elected he would fire the college president. Bennett should have been convicted of an earlier textbook conspiracy charge, Gilmer scolded. Judge Oras A. Shaw of Tulsa had dropped the indictment against Bennett, and Bennett retorted to Gilmer that there was no evidence to prove that he had been connected with illegal textbook revisions.[12]

Striking deeper into the heart of the so-called machine, Gilmer screamed that Jones was betrayed by Turner and Kerr. Gilmer asserted that on July 2, the day of the primary, at a time when Jones was running second to Turner, Kerr summoned Jones to the governor's office and forced his withdrawal and support of Turner. When Jones refused, he was supposedly bound, gagged, and kept in seclusion for nine days until the results of the voting offically removed him from his early second place lead in the primary. Jones had been Kerr's favorite candidate, Gilmer argued, but when it became apparent that Turner would poll the most votes, Kerr switched his loyalties. Kerr's supposed objective was to defeat Gilmer even if it meant abandoning Jones and favoring Turner. Kerr allegedly reasoned that if Jones ran second and declined to contest Turner in a runoff primary then Gilmer would have no chance. Kerr and Jones emphatically stated that the incident was untrue and that Jones was out of the running at the time it was to have taken place. Holding to his story, Gilmer produced his personally signed affidavit swearing that Jones had phoned him at home pleading for Gilmer to remain in the race.[13]

Turner countered with his original programs and branded Gilmer as a pawn of the "money-bag Tulsa Republicans" who were using Gilmer to destroy the Democratic Party in Oklahoma. Turner held that these Republicans would likely throw their support to Olney F. Flynn of Tulsa, the Republican candidate for governor, even if Gilmer won the Democratic nomination. Seventy-five percent of all of Gilmer's backing came from Republican dominated areas of the state, Turner exhorted. Slandering his opponent further, Turner said that Gilmer had summoned George S. Long, a relative of the once powerful Huey P. Long of Louisiana, to participate in the Tulsan's campaign. Apparenly, Long had been seen propagandizing for Gilmer in a large truck equipped with a public address system.[14]

The Gilmer indictments and Turner's rebuttals did not create overwhelming strength for Turner as some had hoped. Newspaper headlines read: "Turner Still Holds an Edge, But Runoff Is No Walkaway." Gilmer made definite progress in areas of the state where he had polled far behind in the primary. The flamboyance of the podium must have been confusing for many Democratic voters who, in spite of the falsehoods or truths, cast 169,397 votes for Gilmer and 194,311 for Turner.[15]

The Democrats in September organized a campaign caravan which stumped the entire state in preparation for the general election in November. Turner denied Flynn's allegations that he was a multimillionaire affiliated with the Democratic machine. Republicans held that Turner would be a pawn in the hands of many powerful lawmakers, because he cleverly avoided any attacks on the people who would one day help to make his plan a workable reality—the "legislative oligarchy." On election day in November, 227,426 people voted for Flynn and 259,491 chose Turner, the winner.[16]

Turner emphasized his complete program in his January, 1947, inaugural address, stressing foremost his reorganization plans for the state highway and tax commissions. The legislature

Candidate Turner, his wife and mother, are pictured here voting for governor in 1946 (Mrs. Roy J. Turner, Oklahoma City, Oklahoma).

was quick to approve the reorganization plans, which raised the salaries of the chairman and the two members of the tax commission. Their terms were also staggered in an effort to make the group as non-political and serviceable as possible.[17]

Another theme receiving strong attention in Turner's inaugural address was his ardent belief that agriculture and industry would be greatly stimulated in Oklahoma through a more centralized network of highways and decreased taxes. One of Turner's favorite examples of potential industrial growth was movie production. Turner's hobby was writing and singing country and western songs, and he believed that the romantic, idealized old West could be portrayed in Oklahoma. It was often difficult to amuse the governor with this type of music, because he would compulsively attempt to perform for the entertainers and the audience. This was Turner's primary escape from the tensions of life while serving as governor.[18]

With the task of informing the legislature and the people of his plan for improving Oklahoma, Turner faced another crucial task at the onset of his administration. Competent advisers and assistants, and a shrewd selection of gubernatorial appointments to state agencies were a necessity for the success of his program. Turner often moved at a snail's pace, as he arduously calculated who would be the best person for each vacant post. Harry W. "Coach" McNeil of Oklahoma City, a man who served as one of Turner's intimate political confidants, accompanied the governor to Washington, D. C., on many occasions. These trips to the nation's capitol were extremely important, for it was there that Turner bargained for federal grants to support his road programs. Turner's prestige increased as a result of his conferences with top officials in Washington. He even received an invitation, which he declined, from President Harry S. Truman to become secretary of agriculture in 1949.[19]

Turner's executive secretary and close adviser, William Forrest McIntire, was another fellow traveler to Washington, although McIntire was carefully scrutinized before he was fully accepted by the governor. When McIntire was new on the job, Turner and McNeil left Oklahoma City, leaving the entire executive office management to McIntire, who apparently did an excellent job, for he remained with Turner four years. Tilford T. Johnson was another associate whom Turner tested thoroughly, for Johnson worked several months as press secretary before he was paid. Apparently the governor was determining both Johnson's loyalty to stay with the job and his courage to threaten to quit if not rewarded; Turner soon found both qualities. Leon Shipp, Turner's attorney, and Alice MacElroy, his personal secretary, proved invaluable for Turner's administrative requirements. Although his day sometimes did not begin until almost 10:00 a.m., he and his staff would often work until 7:00 or 8:00 p.m. Long hours and warm friendships matured into romance for some of Turner's staff. Johnson and MacElroy eventually were married, and in due time McIntire and Hazel M. McKinnis, a former secretary in the office, also married.[20]

Teamwork and continuous individual conferences with legislators won successes. Reorganization of the tax commission, the game and fish commission, and the planning and resources board were accomplished smoothly, but some of Turner's program would not go unchallenged. Although the 1949 legislature readily passed Turner's highway plan, critics of the proposal continued to criticize the highway commission's use of the money. Tulsa newspapers regularly blasted what it considered unfair allotments of highway money, while Turner fought back with charges that the First and Fifth Oklahoma Congressional Districts were greedy and uncooperative.[21]

The 1947 session also passed the initial Turner Turnpike bill, but this feat was only the beginning of a long turnpike struggle for Turner. The project lacked financing and was opposed by many small towns between the proposed northeast and southwest gates at Tulsa and Oklahoma City. Bristow and Stroud were but two Oklahoma towns which complained that their tourist money would disappear since the turnpike was planned to bypass them. The charges of the small towns were joined by Albert S. Goss, the master of the National Grange, who claimed that the cost of the toll would cripple the farm economy. The National Association of Motor Bus Operators, the American Farm Bureau, and the American Automobile Association also headed Turner's list of critics.[22]

Tenseness developed when the 1949 legislature was faced with killing or reinstating the bill which had created the possibility of the Turner Turnpike. Except for an early contribution of $48,000 by Oklahoma City, Tulsa, and Sapulpa, Oklahoma, businessmen, private backers of the project were nonexistent in 1949, and federal loans were being held up by quarrels over costs. Turner managed, however, to convince the 1949 legislature that the project was feasible, and in the last year of his term construction began on the turnpike. The road, the third experiment of its kind west of the Mississippi River, was financed totally with revenue bonds purchased by out-of-state firms.[23]

Rivaling the turnpike bill in the 1947 session of the legislature for the most controverial proposal, was the reorganization of

In December of 1950, Governor Turner, shown on the far right, and the members of the Oklahoma Turnpike Authority broke ground for the proposed eighty-six mile toll road between Oklahoma City and Tulsa. The highway was later named the Turner Turnpike (Oklahoma Publishing Company).

the Oklahoma Board of Education. The bill also consolidated school districts having fewer than thirteen students. Moreover, a one cent gasoline tax was adopted for county commissioners to build all-weather roads on school bus routes. Strong objections came from citizens of rural school areas who feared the loss of their autonomous districts. The proposal cost Turner rural support when he ran in the 1954 Democratic primary for the United States Senate.[24]

As Turner had promised, aid was given to many unfortunate and disabled Oklahomans. The lawmakers in 1947 appropriated more than $2 million to finance a state program for veterans between 1947 and 1948, broadened vocational rehabilitation laws, and restored a vocational education division. Laws were passed also in the 1947 legislature which provided training centers for crippled children. But more dramatically the house and senate overturned the antiquated lunacy law of 1917 with a new mental law which appointed an experienced medical director to the Oklahoma Board of Mental Health, sanctioned the affiliation of mental health clinics with state hospitals, and abolished the practice of defining self-committed persons as insane. The warden of the Oklahoma Penitentiary at McAlester received administrative support in a stand against patronage demands by legislators, which added immensely to the list of reforms for state institutions.[25]

Another feat for Turner during his first legislative session was a $104 million appropriation, an increase of $29 million allotted over the previous two years. Yet the state income tax was reduced one third, setting the stage for Turner's encourage-ment to industrial growth. Although higher education funds were increased, the amount appropriated was $8 million, which was less than the amount requested by the schools. State mental institutions were among the most fortunate recipients, receiving double their allotment for the two previous years.[26]

During his first year as governor, Turner made strides toward the fulfillment of his campaign promises by employing political leadership within the state government and within his own party. He definitely rejected the prospect that Kerr be allowed to retain the position of national committeeman for the Democrats if the ex-governor ran for the United States Senate in 1948. Turner had put a check on Kerr and proved that he could play the game of politics and keep his word at the same time.[27]

Turner learned also that keeping his word and funding bills was often very difficult. With the legislature out of session in 1948, he spent a great deal of time in Washington haggling over funds promised by the United States Public Roads Administra-tion. Money pledged in May of 1948 was delayed until the following September, when nearly $9 million was finally rationed to the state.[28]

Seeking money from the federal government was not Turner's only association with Washington officials. Throughout his

Governor Turner met with President Harry S. Truman in September of 1948 at the White House to discuss the presidential campaign (Mrs. Roy J. Turner, Oklahoma City, Oklahoma).

term, he earned a large amount of respect and recognition from President Truman. At the Democratic National Convention in Philadelphia, and in an August, 1948, visit to Washington, Turner arranged to become national president of the Truman-Barkley for President Club.[29]

Although Turner was a successful fund raiser and campaigner for the Democratic Party in 1948, one paricular feat deserves special attention. Turner was one Democrat who never gave up hope that Truman would be victorious, even though Thomas E. Dewey, the Republican candidate, was favored by many to win the 1948 race for the presidency. Turner's expectations appeared shattered when Truman's campaign train entered Oklahoma lacking funds. Through private contributions, Turner was able to muster all the money Truman needed to complete his campaign trail. After Truman was elected president, he sent a personal letter to Turner thanking him for his service during the campaign.[30]

Although a dedicated Democrat, Turner was unusually diplomatic politically when he assumed the role of governor. He demonstrated this by greeting Dewey in 1948, although a prominent Democrat, Ernest W. Marland, had refused earlier to greet presidential candidate Herbert Hoover, and Governor Kerr had declined an invitition to meet Dewey during the 1944 presidential race. Thus Turner proved that he was both a loyal Democrat and a gracious representative of his state.[31]

With the 1948 presidential election out of the way, Turner needed to prepare for his second legislature, which would convene in January of 1949. Though accomplishments were behind him, he faced special challenges on funding his programs. Despite these budget problems, he upheld his promise to at least hold the line on taxes. Turner stated the problem in his address to his second legislature: "Either we shall yield to the mounting pressure for greatly expanded governmental services—a course, which would be marked by skyrocketing taxes—or we shall do our utmost to steer a middle course, providing essential services with what resources we have at hand, without destroying the equilibrium of our state tax structure."[32]

Continuing, Turner stressed the need for improving state facilities, although he did not recommend the need for building more. He advised the legislature to delay appropriations for common schools until the federal government pledged its share of money. Yet he asked the session to continue with the reorganization plan to provide for more efficient, centralized control of school districts. His message made further recommendations for the maintenance and progress of state institutions, particularly mental facilities and the public welfare system. In conjunction with his welfare department suggestions, Turner noted the large number of children receiving state aid and requested that abandonment laws for children be strengthened.[33]

With regard to education and research, Turner's speech pushed for salary increases for common school teachers, but at the some time he reminded his listeners that this reward should be based on a teacher's ability and experience. The free textbook pledge made to the people of Oklahoma in the general election of 1946 demanded more money, while higher education required additional funds as well. Turner's specific example was Langston University, in dire need of a certified masters program in education. Turner did not omit pleas for research in agriculture, improvements in vocational training, and aid to conservation. He used the Grand River Dam Authority as a prize example of the benefits to be gained from such endeavors. Joining these projects, he recommended the improvement of state parks and recreational facilities.[34]

In keeping with his campaign promises, Turner pushed hard also in his address to the 1949 legislature for more and better farm-to-market roads. Here and in statements which would follow he blasted county commissioners for their tardiness in submitting projects to the Oklahoma Highway Commission, claiming that they had risked losing federal funds. He further criticized the commissioners' practice of giving road mainte-nance and construction priority to secondary roads. Turner wanted the commissioners to concentrate on major farm-to-market roads within the separate counties.[35]

Turner also developed a new method of funding these road projects. He proposed a one-half cent increase in the gasoline tax which would be earmarked for school and mail routes. He also planned to transfer automobile and farm truck license revenue, previously rationed for school districts, to road construction. With his school district reorganization plan already in effect, money for the newly consolidated districts would come out of the state general fund. This plan drew stubborn rebuttals from a statewide organization, the Oklahoma County Commissioners Association. In January, 1949, meeting with Turner in the Blue Room of the capitol, the commissioners fought to continue giving road maintenance and construction priority to secondary roads, though the future would award victory to Turner.[36]

For Turner, his legislative battles took on a more personal nature when he struck a crippling blow at house member Joseph D. McCarty, who had continually charged that the legislature was rubber stamped. Turner employed an old political maneuver when he directed heads of state departments to dismiss all of McCarty's patronage job holders, including the politician's sister and father. Turner held that McCarty was vindictive because he had not been elected speaker of the house of representatives in 1947, although McCarty had been named chairman of the business and industry committee. Turner's punitive action against McCarty revealed a revengeful but rarely seen personality characteristic. It was assumed that this anger had been partially motivated by McCarty allegedly impersonating the governor in Detroit, Michigan, bars. John W. Russell, Jr., the house speaker pro tempore from Okmulgee County, came to McCarty's defense, stating that the incidents in Detroit were merely acts of jest, but Russell apparently was not able to curtail the governor's actions against McCarty. Robert O. Cunningham, a representative from Oklahoma County, also witnessed a purge of his patronage employees at the request of state senator John H. Jarman, Jr., of Oklahoma City. To ease subsequent tensions between Turner and the lawmakers over the patronage issue, Turner appointed James H. Arrington of Stillwater, the state Democratic chairman, to serve as a contact man between the governor and the representatives. Early in February, 1949, Turner and Arrington hosted a party for house and senate members, which took place at the Skirvin Hotel, and seemed to sooth many troubled politicians.[37]

Other complaints, however, developed from the problem of financing Turner's many governmental innovations. He met with a joint conference of legislative leaders early in May, 1949, and agreed to balance the budget and adjourn without considering any more tax increases or a special bond election. Turner, who had at one point advocated a bond election providing for new state buildings, had apparently changed his mind and went along with the consensus opinion of the meeting. In rejecting further taxation, the legislative leaders

Governor and Mrs. Turner spent frequent weekends at their Hereford Heaven Ranch near Sulphur, Oklahoma, to escape the pressures of office (Mrs. Roy J. Turner, Oklahoma City, Oklahoma).

stifled any attempts to consider the repeal of prohibition. William Logan, president pro tempore of the senate, and Walter Billingsley, speaker of the house of representatives, sharply contested these decisions.[38]

Turner invited the two men to join him on his regular Sunday afternoon radio broadcast, where he said that a bond issue would be a burden on the people of Oklahoma. He continued that money was currently available to allow for limited construction and modernization of some state buildings. Billingsley agreed with the governor's idea that industry would suffer from tax increases, but reminded the radio audience that the bond proposal imposed no new taxes. Billingsley concluded that the bonds, first suggested by Turner, would have been retired by two cents of the cigarette tax, and faulted the chief executive for relenting on his original idea. Although Logan cautiously lamented the use of alcohol, he said that as long as the beverage was being consumed, its sale should be legalized and taxed. The legislature had voted for an enlarged common school bill, including a raise in teachers' salaries, Logan emphasized, but pointed out that prohibition needed to be repealed to create funds for these measures. The radio program must have had some effect, for before the 1949 legislative session adjourned it sanctioned a special election for the building bond issue and the repeal of prohibition.[39]

By and large, Turner won a victory, for most of the bickering was over securing money. His free textbook pledge was underwritten by the common school bill, which took $50 million out of the total appropriated amount of $142.5 million. The legislature, however, flatly rejected his hope for more reorganization of school districts and his suggestion that school district bus transportation be taxed. In rebuffing the legislature in June, 1949, when it adjourned, he killed ten of its bills by pocket veto, two of which were a $40,000 annual appropriation for city junior colleges and a forty hour work week for state employees.[40]

Turner's victories for state institutions were uneven. Mental and higher education institutions did not get money equal to the amount requested, although they did receive an increase over the amount granted by the previous legislature. The children's code, creating a crippled children's commission, was another progressive accomplishment for the administration. The governor won bills for an integrated state purchasing system and for a classified system for prisoners in state penal institutions. Three members, however, of the Oklahoma Board of Public Affairs were exonerated of charges of violating state purchasing laws, and authorities at Central State Hospital were exonerated from involvement in the death of a patient. Overall, only a small step was made toward protecting and encouraging many frustrated and needy people in Oklahoma.[41]

Turner's greatest triumphs were in road building, for $13 million was severed from the general fund for the highway department, while direction of the farm-to-market roads program went to the highway department. He also won battles for laws against overloaded trucks and for an enforced speed limit on state highways. When challenged by the job of organizing efficient road construction, Turner emerged a champion.[42]

The remaining govermental decisions were left to the voters, who decided to give $36 million to state institutions at a special bond issue election held in September, 1949. The measure was designed primarily to aid mental hospitals and eleemosynary institutions. Although some controversy occurred at a special legislative session held late in 1949 over the bond issue appropriations for educational facilities, the mentally ill eventually received the lion's share.[43]

Turner's last legislative session was at an end and, as he began the final year of his term, he once again became more involved in national issues as he had in the presidential election of 1948. He again provided hardy support for President Truman and the anti-communist campaign in the United States, when he expressed a desire to reopen World War II airforce bases in Oklahoma. On several occasions he promoted defense training in the state, emphasizing that the American Red Cross must be improved by increasing the number of instructors participating in the first aid training program. He urged Oklahomans to contribute to the international fund raising drive against communism launched in September of 1950 by General Dwight D. Eisenhower, ex-World War II commander, and General Lucius D. Clay, former military governor of Germany. Turner exhorted that United States citizens had taken freedom for granted and that all residents should show their appreciation for democracy by signing the Freedom Scroll, a document enumerating the civil rights of all people. While working with President Truman for democracy, Turner won national recognition by becoming one of the top contenders for the post of

national director of the civil defense office of the National
Security Resources Board. He removed himself from the list,
however, stating that his first obligation was as governor of
Oklahoma.[44]

Turner was decidedly opinionated about the 1950 primaries
in Oklahoma. He declared that Mabel Basset, a former commissioner of state charities, had mistakenly charged that the
state penal and eleemosynary institutions remained in fearful
condition. Basset contested Buck Cook of Osage County, the
incumbent commissioner of state charities and corrections, who
defeated Basset in both the primary and runoff primary. Also in
the primary, the people voted for a workman's compensation
law benefitting the dependents of people who died as a result of
job injuries. In doing so, Oklahomans sounded their disapproval
of Turner's veto of a similar measure during the 1949 legislative
session. The general election of 1950 proved, nevertheless, that
the people of Oklahoma agreed with Turner's highway
programs, because voters rejected two state questions abolishing the eight member highway commission and the gasoline and
license tax.[45]

Johnston Murray, the secretary of the state school land
commission, grabbed the Democratic nomination for governor
in the runoff primary from William O. Coe. In the gubernatorial
race, Murray then faced Jo O. Ferguson, a Pawnee newspaper
editor, who promised to destroy the state highway commission.
Turner lent his voice to Murray and a Democratic victory in
November. In his addresses supporting Murray and the
Democrats, Turner emphasized having a legislature and a
governor belonging to the Democratic Party. In defending this
concept, the governor asserted that there would be less disagreement among people of the same party, making for a
quieter and more productive government.[46]

Before Murray took office, the Future Farmers of America
and 4-H groups sponsored a four-hour testimonial farewell
banquet honoring the retiring governor. Turner was deeply
touched, and in his mild, humble manner, he offered the best
response he could think of—a simple "thank you." Murray was
present at the banquet, and before the evening was over,

For years Governor Turner hosted and honored 4-H Club and Future Farmers of America members at his Hereford Heaven Ranch near Sulphur, Oklahoma (Western History Collections, University of Oklahoma).

Turner offered the governor-elect his best wishes and warned him to "sharpen his axe." Turner explained that being governor was like the tedious chore of chopping wood, and that his axe was very dull by that time. Turner left office as one of the most popular governors the state had ever produced, and many people continued to admire him.[47]

Apparently Turner's four years in office did not tire him enough to forget other political ambitions, because his most newsworthy feat while in retirement was his bid in 1954 for the United States Senate. Kerr, his opponent, was a wealthier and more vibrant personality who used his vigorous intellect and charisma while he stumped the rural areas of Oklahoma. Kerr was a non-drinking Baptist who vigorously opposed repeal of prohibition, and because of this he established considerable harmony with the country people. In addition to the drinking issue in 1954, field crops were poor, causing farmers to vote even more heavily for Kerr. Turner, who had a good chance to capture the rural vote, did not work as hard as Kerr. One legislator who supported Turner's race for the United States Senate told "Coach" McNeil, Turner's political adviser, he needed desperately to stump much more in the country if he planned to win. This advice fell on deaf ears or came too late, for Turner lost to Kerr in the primary.[48]

After selling his oil interests to Harper in 1955, Turner busied himself with farming and the cattle business. He sold his Hereford Heaven Ranch to Winthrop Rockefeller in 1963, marking the end of a significant era in his life, including his cherished weekend trips to the country. He continued to operate a 2,800 acre farm in LeFlore County on the Arkansas River, and soon became a partner in Frontier Feed Yards of Guymon, Oklahoma. This feedlot operation was a powerful industrial concern with a 44,000 head capacity.[49]

Turner was honored for his achievements and contributions to Oklahoma's development when he was initiated into the Oklahoma Hall of Fame in 1957. Civic work was a major concern throughout his life. He displayed pride in Oklahoma's history when as governor he helped the Oklahoma Historical Society secure the papers of Major General Amiel W. Whipple, who in 1853 surveyed a railroad route across what would become Oklahoma. Whipple had recorded in much detail his impressions of the area and its future. Turner's enthusiasm for Oklahoma's heritage continued when he served as a trustee for the National Cowboy Hall of Fame and Western Heritage Center. In fact, he was instrumental in securing this national shrine for Oklahoma City. True to his nationalistic beliefs, Turner also served as state chairman of the Crusade for Freedom and the Young Men's Christian Association youth and government programs.[50]

A suite in the Skirvin Tower Hotel in Oklahoma City provided comfortable living for Turner and his wife following his service as governor. He would sit for hours in the hotel's Tower Club and reminisce with friends. He deeply enjoyed these times with such people as Ruby and Dan W. James, owners of the Skirvin Tower Hotel, and Ann and Victor Crowell, also residents. Turner and his wife were invited often to the Crowell's suite to laugh and talk, but before long, recalled Mrs. Crowell, "Roy would pull out his guitar and play country and western songs. He didn't sing very well, but we all liked him so much it didn't matter."[51] In his older years, he was still the quiet person he had always been, showing a flare of exuberance when he felt the urge to sing.[52]

Turner and his wife moved out of their Skirvin Tower Hotel suite in the middle 1960s but they resided in Oklahoma City until June 11, 1973, when poor general health and a brain tumor took the seventy-nine year old former governor. He was buried in Fairlawn Cemetery in Oklahoma City. Not long before his death, a monument marking his birthplace was dedicated near Kendrick. He returned for the occasion to deliver a message recalling the highlights of his administration.[53]

Friends have said that no one ever wanted to be governor of Oklahoma any more than Turner. Perhaps it is the ambition of some who are born into poverty to challenge their environment. If this is true, then Turner was one such person, because he became both wealthy and powerful. He employed the benefits which these qualities gave him to serve both himself and his state.[54]

Turner was a progressive Democrat who recognized the existence of a highly bureaucratic system of state government and tried to maximize its efficiency through the consolidation of state agencies and a better transportation network. His administration helped to catapult the farmer into a position where he could cope with the demands of the rapidly industrializing agrarianism of the time. Most of his constituents recognized the need for such changes and praised him for his efforts. But there were those who fought the future, and because of this there were those who opposed him.

Turner's aid to people long neglected by public officials is evidence that he could mix his pragmatism with a humanitarian outlook. But the knowledge that only partial strides could be made toward better facilities for mental patients, prisoners, and abandoned children presented frustrations for Turner to face. Taking refuge from these disappointments and from the harassments of the governor's office, he sometimes escaped behind the mask of the singing, lonesome cowboy. This was in fact the person he might have been, had he not deeply desired to be the person he became.

ENDNOTES

[1] Glen Vaughn Interview, Oklahoma City, Oklahoma, June 11, 1976.

[2] Ibid.

[3] Jessica E. Turner Interview, Oklahoma City, Oklahoma, June 12, 1976.

[4] Roy P. Stewart Interview, Oklahoma City, Oklahoma, June 18, 1976.

[5] Ibid.

[6] Jessica E. Turner Interview, June 12, 1976.

[7] Ibid.

[8] James H. Arrington Interview, Oklahoma City, Oklahoma, June 10, 1976; Roy P. Stewart Interview, June 21, 1976.

[9] Daily Oklahoman (Oklahoma City, Oklahoma), January 14, 1947, pp. 1-2.

[10] Ibid., June 12, 1946, pp. 1-2, June 16, 1946, p. A-18, June 9, 1946, pp. A-1-2, 21.

[11] Lee Slater, comp., Directory of Oklahoma, 1975 (Oklahoma City: Oklahoma Election Board, 1975), pp. 479-480; Daily Oklahoman, July 3, 1946, p. 1, July 7, 1946, p. A-10, July 14, 1946, p. A-1.

[12] Daily Oklahoman, July 7, 1946, p. A-10, July 9, 1946, p. 5, July 6, 1946, p. 2.

[13] Tulsa World (Tulsa, Oklahoma), July 9, 1946, pp. 1-2, 4; Daily Oklahoman, July 19, 1946, p. 14, July 17, 1946, p. 3, July 16, 1946, p. 1.

[14] Daily Oklahoman, July 16, 1946, p. 2, July 10, 1946, p. 5.

[15] Ibid., July 14, 1946, p. A-1; Slater, comp., Directory of Oklahoma, 1975, pp. 479-480.

[16] Daily Oklahoman, September 1, 1946, p. A-14, October 1, 1946, p. 2; Slater, comp., Directory of Oklahoma, 1975, p. 482.

[17] Daily Oklahoman, January 14, 1947, pp. 1-2.

[18] Ibid., January 14, 1947, pp. 1-2, January 11, 1948, pp. D-1, D-4; Dan W. James Interview, Oklahoma City, Oklahoma, June 22, 1976; Ann Crowell Farris Interview, Oklahoma City, Oklahoma, June 22, 1976; Tilford T. Johnson Interview, Oklahoma City, Oklahoma, June 14, 1976.

[19] Tilford T. Johnson Interview, June 14, 1976; William F. McIntire Interview, Oklahoma City, Oklahoma, June 14, 1976.

[20] Tilford T. Johnson Interview, June 14, 1976.

[21] Daily Oklahoman, January 14, 1947, pp. 1-2; Tulsa Tribune (Tulsa, Oklahoma), October 3, 1950, p. 34; Daily Oklahoman, October 14, 1950, p. 7, October 3, 1950, p. 8.

[22] Tilford T. Johnson Interview, June 14, 1976; Daily Oklahoman, December 26, 1948, p. A-20.

[23] Roy P. Stewart Interview, June 18, 1976.

[24] Daily Oklahoman, January 11, 1948, pp. 1, 4; Roy P. Stewart Interview, June 18, 1976.

[25] Daily Oklahoman, May 8, 1947, p. 3, May 9, 1947, p. 6, June 1, 1947, p. A-10, January 11, 1948, pp. D-1, D-4, August 11, 1947, p. 5.

[26] Ibid., January 11, 1948, pp. D-1, D-4.

[27] Ibid., October 26, 1947, p. A-7.

[28] Roy P. Stewart Interview, June 18, 1976; Tilford T. Johnson Interview, June 14, 1976; James H. Arrington Interview, June 10, 1976; Daily Oklahoman, September 1, 1948, p. 11.

[29] William F. McIntire Interview, June 14, 1976; Tilford T. Johnson Interview, June 14, 1976; Daily Oklahoman, August 27, 1948, p. 30; Roy P. Stewart Interview, June 18, 1976.

[30] James H. Arrington Interview, June 10, 1976; Tilford T. Johnson Interview, June 14,

1976; William F. McIntire Interview, June 14, 1976.

³¹ *Daily Oklahoman*, September 17, 1948, p. 1, October 14, 1948, p. 1.

³² Message to the Legislature, January 9, 1949, p. 3, Governor Roy J. Turner Administrative File, Archives and Records Division, Oklahoma Department of Libraries, Oklahoma City, Oklahoma.

³³ *Ibid.*, pp. 4, 5, 6, 9.

³⁴ *Ibid.*, pp. 6, 10, 11.

³⁵ *Ibid.*, pp. 7, 8; *Daily Oklahoman*, March 27, 1949, p. A-9.

³⁶ *Daily Oklahoman*, March 27, 1949, p. A-9, January 12, 1949, p. 19; Message to the Legislature, January 9, 1949, p. 8, Governor Roy J. Turner Administrative File, Archives and Records Division, Oklahoma Department of Libraries.

³⁷ *Daily Oklahoman*, January 25, 1949, p. 2, January 29, 1949, p. 1; William F. McIntire Interview, June 14, 1976; *Daily Oklahoman*, January 30, 1949, p. A-15, February 1, 1949, p. 2, February 2, 1949, pp. 1, 2.

³⁸ *Daily Oklahoman*, May 8, 1949, pp. 1, 2.

³⁹ *Ibid.*

⁴⁰ *Ibid.*, June 12, 1949, p. A-8, May 29, 1949, pp. 1-2.

⁴¹ *Ibid.*, May 7, 1949, p. A-7, May 29, 1949, pp. 1-2.

⁴² *Ibid.*

⁴³ *Ibid.*, November 27, 1949, p. A-1, December 11, 1949, p. A-1.

⁴⁴ *Ibid.*, July 28, 1950, p. 13, September 3, 1950, p. A-11, September 23, 1950, p. 6, September 16, 1950, p. 7, October 6, 1950, p. 5, October 8, 1950, p. A-3.

⁴⁵ *Ibid.*, July 24, 1950, p. 1; Slater, comp., *Directory of Oklahoma, 1975*, pp. 486, 532-533.

⁴⁶ Slater, comp., *Directory of Oklahoma, 1975*, pp. 485-486; *Daily Oklahoman*, October 31, 1950, p. 9.

⁴⁷ *Daily Oklahoman*, December 17, 1950, p. B-6; Roy P. Stewart Interview, June 18, 1976.

⁴⁸ Otis Sullivant, "Rich Man's Race," *Nation*, Vol. CLXXVIII, No. 26 (June 26, 1954), pp. 542-543; Harold Lavine, "Dollar Derby," *Newsweek*, Vol. XLIII, No. 21 (May 24, 1954), pp. 26-27; James H. Arrington Interview, June 10, 1976.

⁴⁹ Jessica E. Turner Interview, June 12, 1976.

⁵⁰ *Ibid.*; "Minutes of the Meeting of the Board of Directors of the Oklahoma Historical Society, January 26, 1950," *The Chronicles of Oklahoma*, Vol. XXVII, No. 1 (Spring, 1950), p. 117; Muriel H. Wright and George H. Shirk, "The Journal of Lieutenant A. W. Whipple," *The Chronicles of Oklahoma*, Vol. XXVII, No. 2 (Summer, 1950), p. 235; Jessica E. Turner Interview, June 12, 1976.

⁵¹ Ann Crowell Farris Interview, June 22, 1976.

⁵² Jessica E. Turner Interview, July 6, 1976; Roy P. Stewart Interview, June 18, 1976.

⁵³ James H. Arrington Interview, June 10, 1976; Tilford T. Johnson Interview, June 14, 1976; Roy P. Stewart Interview, June 18, 1976.

⁵⁴ Roy P. Stewart Interview, June 18, 1976.

Johnston Murray

Governor of Oklahoma, 1951-1955

By Jim L. Myers

Johnston Murray

Johnston Murray described his term as governor of Oklahoma to a writer for the *Saturday Evening Post* as "four hectic, often frustrating years." Murray explained that in "a way, I felt good. Wasn't I leaving the toughest governorship in the land? Still I experienced no sense of relief. I kept on fuming about the staggering maze of unsolved problems which shame my state and hold it in the category of the retarded."[1]

Murray's reflections, which appeared in the *Saturday Evening Post* just a little over three months after he left office, helped deteriorate further his political position in Oklahoma. His standing among the political leaders of the state appeared to have slipped during his last year in office, and his farewell message to the state legislators was, in his own words, "a rawhiding for their cheap political greeds, their surrender to clutching lobbies, their reckless extravagance—in brief, for all the faithless behavior which had consigned our potentially great state to economic distress."[2]

Some would say that Murray had come by this attitude bordering on irascibility naturally. He was, after all, the second son of William H. "Alfalfa Bill" Murray, who had preceded him as governor of Oklahoma exactly twenty years earlier. Stories concering the administration of the elder Murray, an independent and strong-willed executive, will long circulate as both fact and legend. The younger Murray spoke many times of the large influence that his father had over his early life. This same attitude of respect was also present when Murray talked about his mother, Mary Alice Hearrell Murray, a part Chickasaw Indian. Mrs. Murray was the niece of Douglas H. Johnston, once governor of the Chickasaw Nation, and it was in the Johnston home, called the White House, at Emet in Johnston County, that Murray was born on July 21, 1902, when the area was still part of the Chickasaw Nation.

During Murray's early childhood, his family, which included four boys and one girl, lived in Tishomingo, where Murray attended public schools. Later, when his father represented an Oklahoma congressional district in the United States House of Representatives, he attended public school in Washington, D.C. In 1924, Murray graduated from Murray State College, where, according to his father, he had been an excellent football player. Murray had married his first wife, Marian Draughon of Sulphur, in 1923, and they had one son, Johnston Jr. After six years of marriage, the couple divorced, and Murray married Willie Roberta Emerson on May 1, 1933.

As a young man, Murray worked at various jobs. While still in his twenties, he was employed by a newspaper as a printer as well as a news reporter. In 1924, he accompanied his father to Bolivia, a country in west-central South America, where the elder Murray established an agricultural colony in order to preserve pioneer life that had been so important to the early development of the United States. The younger Murray spent four years in Bolivia, where he became proficient in Spanish, but the colonization attempt eventually failed. When he returned to the United States, Murray worked in the oil and gas fields of Oklahoma in positions from roustabout to plant manager. During World War II, he was placed in charge of several state trade schools in Oklahoma, which trained men to work in munitions plants, and later became personnel director for the

Douglas Aircraft Company in Oklahoma City. Murray continued his formal education by attending night school and received the law degree from Oklahoma City University in 1947.[3]

Before being elected governor of Oklahoma, Murray held several political positions in the state. He served as Democratic chairman of the Oklahoma Eighth Congressional District as well as chairman of the Democratic organizations in Kay and Oklahoma counties. He was also chairman of the Oklahoma Election Board, and in 1946 became secretary of the Oklahoma Land Commission.

Murray announced his intention of seeking the Democratic nomination for governor so that the announcement would reach the newspapers on his late mother's birthday, January 9, 1950. From the start, it was evident that economy was to be the keynote of his campaign. In his first speech, following his father's advice to deliver it "any place South of [the] Canadian," Murray told a Tishomingo audience that the cost of running the state government, which he said had increased from $86 million to $240 million in the preceding twelve years, could be reduced.[4]

The aides of the Murray campaign had one problem that other gubernatorial candidates did not have to face, and that was how to deal with the image of Murray's father, Alfalfa Bill. The elder Murray had created a stir in the Democratic Party in 1936 by refusing to support Franklin D. Roosevelt for president. It was inevitable that Murray would be compared to his father; indeed, Frank P. Douglass, an Oklahoma City attorney and one of Murray's opponents for the Democratic nomination, made sure the voters were reminded of the former governor's political indiscretions. At the same time that he was a potential liability, the elder Murray was also a potential asset, for the Murray name still had great drawing power among state voters. Murray decided that his father was more of an asset than a liability, and as he campaigned across the state, he would remind voters that he was Bill Murray's son. Obviously, the strategy worked; Douglass failed to make it to the runoff primary, as he ran third in the primary ahead of Phil Ferguson, a Woodward rancher and former congressman, but behind Murray and William O. Coe, an Oklahoma City attorney.[5]

By the time Murray had earned a spot in the runoff primary, his campaign coffers needed replenishing. William C. Doenges, a Tulsa auto dealer, was his principal financial backer and would eventually contribute $300,000 to the campaign. More money, however, was needed; it took $100,000 just to finance a state-wide billboard campaign showing Murray and his "Just Plain Folks" slogan. Believing that campaign contributions arrive only when people think you do not need them, Doenges devised a stratagem to meet the financial needs of the campaign. He borrowed $150,000 from a Tulsa bank and took half of the money to Oklahoma City, where he deposited it with a banker who had political connections, thus giving the impression that the Murray campaign had really caught on and was well financed. When the word spread that Murray did not need money, many people offered it.

The same plan, although on a much smaller scale, worked in other cities. Doenges accompanied Murray on his speaking tours, and after Murray had delivered his speech, Doenges, who had brought along $5,000 in cash, visited with the townspeople and asked for contributions. He then took his $5,000 and whatever he had collected in town to the local banker and asked for a cashier's check, again suggesting that Murray had a large following across the state.[6]

The real story of the runoff primary, however, was the charges made by Murray's opponent, Coe, who promised to take "the skin, hide and hair off Johnston Murray."[7] To make good his promise, Coe used the divorce proceedings filed by Murray's first wife to accuse Murray of child desertion. Murray responded by having his former wife formally refute Coe's charges and announce her support of his candidacy. Johnston Jr., the child Murray was accused of deserting, also actively campaigned for his father. Coe, however, was not finished; he also accused Murray of being a draft-dodger during World War II. To this charge, Murray answered that he had resigned his commission in the Oklahoma National Guard in 1938 and had asked to be allowed to reenlist after the United States became involved in World War II. His request, Murray explained, had been denied due to his age.[8]

Johnston Murray, right, received the oath of office as governor on January 9, 1951, from his father, William H. Murray, who had served as Oklahoma's governor exactly twenty years earlier (Western History Collections, University of Oklahoma).

The bitter campaign did not end with the runoff primary, which Murray won by only 1,009 votes. Coe charged the Murray backers with fraud and petitioned the state election board for recount in all seventy-seven counties in the state. To emphasize and dramatize his point, Coe carried the money required by law to ask for a recount to the state election board in a burlap sack. The results of the recount, which was the state's first complete recount, still gave Murray a 962 vote lead.[9]

Following the bitter contest between Coe and Murray, the general election was calm. The Republican Party nominee was Jo O. Ferguson, a newspaper man from Pawnee. Murray continued to emphasize his two major issues—economy in government and no new taxes—and was elected, receiving 329,308 votes to 313,205 for Ferguson and 1,763 for the Independent Party candidate, Mickey Harrell of Oklahoma City. On January 9, 1951, Murray was given the oath of office by his father.[10]

The most controversial issue during Murray's first year and possibly his entire term developed despite the fact that Murray and the legislature agreed on it. That issue was the bill passed by the legislature in 1951 and signed into law by Murray requiring all state employees to take a loyalty oath. Murray said that even though "there's certainly a minimum of communists in Oklahoma," he favored the oath because it would "alert the people to the things that might creep up on them."[11]

The controversy over the law stemmed mainly from its provisions requiring signers to swear they had not been a member of a communist organization within the past five years and would take up arms in defense of the United States. Concerned about the legality of the bill, Murray had asked the legislature to recall it for reconsideration, but signed it into law when the senate refused to follow the action of the house of representatives, which had voted to recall it. Opposition to the oath soon resulted, especially at the state colleges and university. The state attorney general declared that parts of the law were unconstitutional, but the Oklahoma Supreme Court disagreed and upheld the oath. The state tried to force those refusing to sign the oath to do so by witholding their salaries. In 1952, however, the United States Supreme Court failed to uphold the state supreme court's decision and ruled unanimously that the oath was unconstitutional. A new law requiring state employees hired after July 1, 1953, to sign a loyalty oath was passed by the legislature in its next regular session in 1953. Although it was designed to apply only to new employees by making the oath a condition of entering employment and not remaining on the state's payroll, the law, in effect, required teachers to sign the oath because they were hired annually. The law was never declared unconstitutional.[12]

The legislature also proposed two amendments to the state constitution during Murray's first year in office. One would allow women to serve on juries, and it was approved by state voters. The second, which would have lowered the state voting age to allow eighteen-year-olds to vote, was defeated.[13]

Two major proposals very important to Murray were also introduced in the legislature in 1951. One was a plan to raise and equalize the assessment of property values throughout the state. By doing this, Murray explained, the state could raise more taxes at the local level for the support of education. The governor's plan aimed at increasing property assessments to 35 percent of their actual value and included provisions whereby the Oklahoma Tax Commission could penalize those counties refusing to comply with the measure by withholding state funds. It was because of this decision by Murray that increases in funds for education should be provided for at the local level that he was considered unfriendly by many state educators. The second proposal would have exempted new industry coming to the state from ad valorem and user taxes on equipment for a period of five years. This measure would encourage new industry to locate in the state, which had been one of Murray's campaign pledges in 1950.[14]

With the introduction of these measures, which Murray supported, it became evident that the governor had little influence over the state legislature. He failed to win support for his plan to raise and equalize property taxes. Bill Logan of Lawton, the senate majority floor leader, stated that the legislature preferred a compromise on the measure that would equalize but not raise property taxes. The measure that would have exempted new industry from certain taxes also failed to win necessary support as it was originally designed, and the legislature passed a weaker version of the bill, which was soon ruled unconstitutional by the state attorney general. The governor also had to yield somewhat on his no-new-tax stand when he signed a bill placing a tax on beer, which provided a large portion of the funds appropriated for education.[15]

The major blow to the governor's leadership, however, came in a different form than non-support for his program. A resolution was approved by the house of representatives whereby the legislature would recess instead of adjourning at the end of the legislative session. This move, if it had been approved by the senate, would have meant that the legislature could be called back into session only by its own leaders or a majority of the members of each house. The governor would have been prevented from calling the legislature into special session.[16]

It became apparent to political observers that the governor was headed for trouble with the legislature. Just three months after Murray took office, a political writer for the *Daily Oklahoman* commented that the governor had "let control of the legislature slip away from him." Rather accurately, this observer predicted that although this development would not mean serious trouble for Murray that year, it could "indicate a hectic time in his second legislature two years hence." The writer commented that the cause for the governor's loss of legislative control stemmed from the lack of any real direction from the chief executive. "Murray's principal trouble," he wrote, "has been lack of follow-through on legislative proposals and contact with the legislature."[17]

Murray did succeed in getting the legislature to agree to the need for a committee to study possible reforms in state government. The Governor's Joint Committee on Reorganization of State Government was formed with twelve members of the legislature to work with twelve citizens. The committee met several times during the non-legislative year of 1952.[18]

Even with the disappointments Murray experienced with the legislature, he appeared to enjoy his role as governor. His stand of no additional taxes won him popular support, and public approval seemed important to him. Besides making the necessary public appearances expected of a governor, Murray and his wife, Willie, invited the public to a series of open houses at the governor's office at the capitol as well as at the executive mansion. However much he enjoyed the glamour of being governor, Murray sought privacy, and it was reported that he was absent from the state more than sixty days during his first year in office. Not all of this time, however, was for private vacations.

Governor Johnston Murray, right, with Democratic President Harry S.
Truman. While governor, Murray actively supported the Democratic Party,
but would break with the party after leaving office (Western History Collec-
tions, University of Oklahoma).

Murray also welcomed the opportunity to represent the state
officially, which he did in 1952, when he made a three-week tour
of several South American countries to promote the 1953
International Petroleum Exposition in Tulsa.[19]

Besides trying to retain popularity with the public, Murray
also strove to remain on safe ground within his own political
party during the 1952 elections. Because he was the son of Bill
Murray, who had not always supported the Democratic Party
ticket, reporters asked the governor about his political choices.
Murray explained that while he might listen to the Dixiecrats,
he would not bolt the Democratic Party as his father had done

earlier. "I owe everything I have done politically to the Democratic party," he said.[20] He actively supported Adlai E. Stevenson, the Democratic nominee for president, and delivered several speeches in support of the Democratic ticket.[21]

Murray's approach to the 1952 legislative elections in Oklahoma also differed significantly from that of his father. Unlike the elder Murray, who took an active role in the elections while governor to seperate, as he put it, the "sheep from the goats," the younger Murray declared early that his would be a "hands off policy."[22] Still, Murray's decision to remain neutral during the elections did not seem to improve his posture with the legislature.

When the legislature convened in 1953, Murray made it clear that economy in government and no additional taxes would remain the theme of his administration. In his first legislative address, in which he seemed to be seeking a harmonious working relationship with the legislature, the governor repreated most of his previous positions. Murray urged the legislature to examine ways to economize the cost of government by consolidating boards and commissions, eliminating unnecessary agencies, doing away with lump-sum appropriations, where possible, and instituting a system whereby the budgetary requests could be checked by an agency other than the one using the requested funds. Again, Murray asked that ad valorem taxes be equalized. Possibly to eliminate opposition which had mounted against the proposal in 1951, he stated that the purpose of such a measure "should not be equalization for additional revenue, but we should attempt to equalize taxes placing the burdens where they justly and properly belong."[23]

Citing the work that the Governor's Joint Committee on Reorganization of State Government had begun, Murray suggested that the legislature extend the committee at least two more years. He also asked that the legislators study ways to eliminate the practice of earmarking funds, which he termed "one of the basic causes of waste and one of the greatest impediments against the practice of real economy." He said also that if any earmarking was justified, however, it was the road users tax.[24]

Probably the most controversial suggestion in Murray's message concerned the reformation of the state's seventy-seven counties. Calling the numerical reduction of the counties inevitable, Murray cited ineffectual government in certain counties and improved transportation permitting more distance between the citizen and his government as reasons to reform the existing county system. He predicted that if the legislature failed to prepare such a constitutional amendment, civic organizations around the state would sponsor an initiative petition to bring about the needed reform.[25]

Despite the harmonious tone of the governor's message to the legislature, it soon became apparent that the relationship between the chief executive and the legislature would be less than friendly. On January 15, 1953, Representative Glen Ham of Pauls Valley introduced into the house of representatives a written motion which stated that the house "does not need any further message from the Governor in order to understand his first message, that this House is in favor of such Government reform as is necessary to give the people of this state economical and efficient government." The house approved the motion as well as one stating that a committee to be known as the Governmental Reform Committee be appointed by the house leadership "to study and recommend a program of governmental reform in connection with the Governor's Message." The motion, however, excluded from study the governor's suggestion to reform the state's counties.[26]

This early reaction to the governor's message was only a mild example of the strained relationship that was to develop between Murray and the legislature. In early March, 1953, the *Daily Oklahoman's* political analyst commented on the deterioration of the governor's standing with the legislature. He said Murray had lost control of his legislative proposals because of ineffective leadership. While acknowledging the governor's determination in his speeches, the political writer explained that Murray failed to exert the necessary influence while measures were still in legislative committee. Also, the analyst said that the governor made the mistake of not letting the legislative leaders know the full meaning of his messages to the legislature. As a result of Murray's lack of action to ensure the passage of his proposals, the analyst noted, legislators questioned the governor's sincerity concerning his suggestions on economy and governmental reform. "The legislators claim it is all talk and no action," he said, "and they know effective economy and reform will come only with a strong governor in control and directing the program."[27]

One power of his office Murray was not reluctant to exercise was that of executive veto. As had occurred in the first legislative year of his administration in 1951, the governor found many measures passed by the 1953 legislature that he could not, for one reason or another, sign into law. Unlike the first legislature he worked with, however, this group of lawmakers was able to override his vetoes. In April, 1953, Murray vetoed three bills which concerned the salaries and mileage paid to officials in only three of the counties, but the bills' sponsors were able to secure the necessary votes to pass all three measures into law over the governor's veto. This action was another example of how strained the relationship had become between Murray and the legislature, which had not voted to override a governor's veto since the administration of Ernest W. Marland in the 1930s. The legislature's action did not deter Murray from further use of the veto. At the end of the legislative session, he vetoed twenty bills and killed sections of others, which cut $890,000 from the amount appropriated by the legislature.[28]

Relations between the chief executive and the legislature worsened, and Murray felt compelled to advise the legislators that there "had been brought to my attention from numerous sources reports that a large number of members of the House have tentatively agreed in writing to prolong the present session until five days after all bills have been delivered to my desk . . . to force the Chief Executive to sign, veto, or allow the bills to become law . . . , and in the case of a veto, to override the veto before the session ends sine die." Murray told the legislators that despite these reports, he would continue to follow his own conscience in acting on the legislation sent to him. He also used this message to urge the house of representatives to lay "aside

frivolities, personalities, and partisan politics, and pass to my
desk those measures . . . [so] that you will now change the
thought in the minds of some of our people that this is the most
costly as well as a 'do-nothing' session."[29]

The legislature did not respond to Murray's plea as far as the
major proposals supported by him were concerned. The
legislature adjourned in 1953 without acting on Murray's plan
to equalize property taxes, and the report from the Governor's
Joint Committee on Reorganization of State Government was
also ignored, as was the proposal to consolidate the counties of
the state. In spite of Murray's protests that the amount was too
high, a common school education bill totaling $63.5 million was
passed unanimously by both houses of the legislature. The
governor delayed action on the measure until after he could
ascertain what public opinion was concerning it. After receiving
over 10,000 letters, most of which supported the bill, Murray
allowed the measure to become law without his signature. As a
result, teachers' salaries rose to $2,400 per year, which
amounted to a total increase of $400 during Murray's four years
in office.[30]

Progress, however, was made in several areas despite the
poor relationship existing between Murray and the legislature.
The governor supported the continuation of the highway
improvement program, and he signed the measures passed by
the legislature which expanded the Oklahoma Turnpike
Authority and made provisions for the possible extension of the
Turner Turnpike, which was completed in 1953, from Tulsa to
the Missouri line. He also approved bills providing for the
possible construction of two additional turnpikes—one from
Oklahoma City north toward Wichita, Kansas, and one from
Oklahoma City south toward Wichita Falls, Texas. A special
election was held in January, 1954, for voters to ballot on the
measures after opponents of the turnpikes secured the necessary
number of signatures on a referendum petition. The measures
were approved by the voters. To reward Murray for his support
of the turnpike program, the legislature decided that whichever
turnpike was completed first, it would be named in his honor.
The turnpike authority could only sell enough bonds, however,

to finance the road from Tulsa to the Missouri line, and when it was completed, the decision was made to name it the Will Rogers Turnpike. Progress was made also on the state's mental health program, especially in the area of protecting the rights of patients, and the legislature passed a law in 1953 establishing the Oklahoma Educational Television Authority.[31]

Possibly because of the legislative progress made during his administration, Murray seemed reluctant to end the 1953 session on a bad note. In his final speech to the legislature that year, he stressed its achievements as well as the disappointments he had experienced concerning his own proposals. "Like most of you," he said to the legislators, "I have had disappointments during this session. . . . But during the past several months of your deliberations, I have also been greatly pleased by your actions many times."[32]

The most interesting aspect of his appearance before the legislature that day, however, had nothing to do with legislation. There had been talk of a Murray candidacy for the United States Senate seat then held by Robert S. Kerr, who was also a former governor. In fact, during Murray's visit to the house of representatives chamber, the house leadership had presented him with a summer Stetson hat so he would be able to "throw a hat in the ring of the next campaign."[33] During his speech, however, Murray failed to make his intentions clear, thus leaving open the possibility of a campaign. In the fall of 1953, he was still not committing himself to the United States Senate race. Speaking to the Oklahoma Retailers Association on October 25, he said that he would make an announcement early in the next year, adding that Kerr would be very hard to beat.[34]

The governor was not the only Murray being offered as a possible candidate for political office in 1954. Reports were also circulating that Murray's wife, Willie, might enter the governor's race to succeed her husband, who was constitutionally barred from serving two consecutive terms in office. In January, 1954, however, Murray issued a statement taking both himself and his wife out of contention for political office that year. He explained that he wanted to devote the rest of his time in office to the development of several plans that he had for the state, including one for the establishment of a water authority that would end the problem of water shortages that had always plagued western Oklahoma. Murray stated that if either he or Mrs. Murray were to run for public office, his plans would become political issues. This undoubtedly would occur, since either Murray or his wife would have to run on the record of the Murray administration, but this possibly was not the only reason Murray decided to forego the United States Senate race. He also realized fully that he was correct in his previous statement—Kerr would be very hard to beat. Kerr had considerable money and strong support within the Democratic Party, while Murray was not wealthy and some of his closest associates, like Doenges, were also supporters of Kerr.[35]

Apparently, Mrs. Murray had no such doubts about her own political fortunes. She was a highly ambitious, intelligent person, who felt herself to be intellectually superior to her husband. It was believed that Murray would never have run for governor if it had not been for his wife's insistence. Now it was her turn, and in May, 1954, several months after her husband had taken them both out of contention for political office, Mrs. Murray launched her campaign for the Democratic nomination for governor. Her program, she said, was "the continued growth of Oklahoma." Mrs. Murray defended her husband's leadership and praised the progress made during his administration. As evidence of this progress, she cited industrial expansion, increased tourism, new road construction, and improvements made in the state's mental health program.[36] Later in her campaign, she promised to put more women in government jobs and raise the minimum salary of teachers from $2,400 to $2,600.[37]

Mrs. Murray's campaign failed to attract much support, and it actually damaged her husband politically. Reports were circulating that pressure was being applied to state employees to gain their support of her campaign. Although pressure was probably applied by using the Murray name, it seemed unlikely that the governor approved or even knew of such tactics. From the start, Murray had been opposed to her entering the campaign.[38]

Governor Johnston Murray, second from left, and a group of men inspecting Halliburton oil-well equipment. Throughout his administration, Murray stressed the need for industrial expansion (Western History Collections, University of Oklahoma).

While his wife's campaign presented him with dilemmas, Murray was quite capable of creating his own political problems. In what was an apparent reversal of his earlier public assessment of the legislature, he attacked the legislature for remaining in session too long in a speech before the Oklahoma Press Association in January, 1954. He described many legislators as being "completely gutless," and in reference to his position on the earmarking of state funds, he attacked the legislature for not having the courage to end the practice. The governor also criticized newsmen for biased reporting of news from the Oklahoma Capitol. Accusing them of omitting things that

Johnston Murray, one of Oklahoma's most traveled governors, arrived in Mexico in 1954 for a good-will tour sponsored by the United States State Department (Western History Collections, University of Oklahoma).

should be made public, Murray said reporters only "look for something political to write about."

James C. Nance, a Purcell newspaper publisher who had served as speaker of the house of representatives during the 1953 legislative session, was in the audience when the governor made his remarks concerning the legislature. Afterward, Nance responded that it "was wholly inappropriate for him to come down here and vent his spleen against other elective officials." Nance, who at the time was considered a potential candidate for governor, called Murray a "do-nothing governor" and a "spineless misnomer."[39]

Political attacks on Murray also resulted when he declared

martial law during the primary of 1954. His decree, affecting five Oklahoma counties—Pittsburg, LeFlore, Cherokee, Adair, and Sequoyah—was made after six persons in that area were charged with the selling and buying of votes. The Oklahoma National Guard was called out to patrol election precincts. Several Democratic candidates, including William O. Coe, Murray's former opponent, accused the governor of issuing the declaration as a publicity stunt to help Mrs. Murray's campaign. Despite the charges, unarmed troops watched the polls during the primary on July 6, without incident. The decree was rescinded before the runoff primary by Lieutenant Governor James E. Berry, a Stillwater banker, who was acting as governor while Murray was out of the state.[40]

As difficult as 1954 appeared for Murray, there were still times of enjoyment for him. As had occurred in the opening year of his administration, he traveled extensively during his last year in office. In July, he attended the National Governors Conference in Lake George, New York. He took pride in the recognition given the state by his role in such meetings. While governor of Oklahoma, he had served as the chairman of the Southern Governors Conference and as a member of the executive committee of the National Governors Conference. Also in 1954, the United States Department of State sponsored Murray on a good-will tour of Mexico.[41]

Before leaving office, Murray had one more opportunity to castigate the legislature for failing to modernize the state's government. Just six days before he was succeeded by Raymond D. Gary, Murray delivered his farewell message to the legislature, which had convened in regular session. He used the occasion to criticize the 1951 and 1953 legislatures for not acting on various proposals supported by him. Failure to reduce the number of counties, end the practice of earmarking state funds, and establish a standard ad valorem tax were among the items cited by Murray in his criticisms.[42]

As frank as the language was in his farewell message, Murray evidently used it merely as a warming-up execise. Even before he left office, he was contacted by the author who would write the article that appeared in the *Saturday Evening Post*. The writer said that he hoped Murray would not be "shocked by the kind of material" he thought would by necessary to interest the magazine's editors, and that he would have to give his honest assessment of the state that would be "positive, hard-hitting, with a point to drive home."[43] When the article appeared, it was titled "Oklahoma is in a Mess!"

The article was described as an expose of how greed and poor govenment had retarded the progress of the state. In it Murray summarized all the problems plaguing the state. He saw the drop in state population as being a result of the lack of jobs, which, he said, could only be solved by attracting new industry. But, said he, the prospective investor "looks at our 4 per cent corporation tax, our jumbled local taxation, which though low, tends to saddle industry with too much of the load; our state income tax, sales tax, our excises, our dry laws and poor roads, our screaming need for legislative reform. At this, the industrialist is apt to belittle himself for having considered Oklahoma at all."[44] The former governor also criticized the practice of earmarking state funds which gave legislators control of only one third of the state's total expenditures. While this practice, continued Murray, allowed favored agencies such as the welfare department to keep "eating high on the hog, the highway department starves and our roads go on crumbling and killing." He went on to attack such govermental shortcomings as the state employment system where 20,000 persons worked under no merit system, the long ballot, overproduction of oil, corrupt county commissioners, whom Murray called "231 little kings in 231 little kingdoms," unnecessary boards and commissions, and inadequate local taxes. According to Murray, these problems caused Oklahoma to be "at least a generation behind the times."[45]

Nothing Murray did while in office caused such an uproar in the state as did his *Saturday Evening Post* article, and no one can say definitely why he decided to write it. By his last year as governor, Murray had likely become very disillusioned politically. From his father, he had learned to feel a deep sense of patriotism, and this made him want very much to do well as governor. He learned, however, that politics in part is a selfish profession, and reform, which he believed was so desperately needed, was not easy to achieve when people were concerned mainly with their own interests. He believed also that money was being passed around in the legislature, and he deplored such practices. Frustration caused by his term in office may have caused him to give his story to the magazine. His public image was also very important to him, as it is to most politicians, and after four years of being second-guessed and called a weak executive, he may have wanted to go out with something more than only the expected farewell address.[46]

In the article, Murray explained in part why he made the decision to write it. He described the people of Oklahoma as lacking the "fiery state patriotism" necessary to bring about important reform. "We get bad government," he said, "because we hold still to be skinned, when we ought to get fighting mad." It seemed that it was Murray's intention to help build some of that state partriotism by forcing Oklahomans to read about their problems in a magazine of national circulation. "Perhaps," he stated, "this article will make Oklahomans mad. If so, a great deal of good could come of it." Murray had not given up; he "swore to keep the faith . . . that in spite of her distresses, Oklahoma must someday become an envied bulwark among the states."[47]

As 1955 brought surprises in Murray's public life, it was also a year for personal problems for the former chief executive. In September, he sued his wife, Willie, for divorce after twenty years of marriage. The proceedings, which were prolonged and bitter, made headlines as Mrs. Murray first fought the divorce and then countersued Murray, charging him with public drunkenness and adultery. Marital problems for the Murrays likely began during the last year of his administration. Murray had been totally opposed to her entering the race for governor in 1954, but Mrs. Murray, who had always been more abitious than the governor, could not be persuaded to stay out of the race. Even though public appearances did not indicate it, her campaign seemed to initiate the breakup of their marriage. The divorce was made final in February, 1956, and later that year, Murray married his third wife, Helen Shutt.[48]

After leaving office, Murray needed to find employment. He was not a wealthy man, and he had not benefitted financially while serving as governor. Nor did he have a position to which he could return, for although he had a law degree, he did not have an established law practice. As was his early life, his years after 1955 were marked by a variety of jobs. Immediately upon leaving office, Murray agreed to become vice-president of Welex Jet Service, an oil well servicing and research organization based in Houston, Texas. In 1957, he resigned from that firm, and in the next year, he took a public relations position with a limousine firm in Fort Worth, Texas. In 1960, Murray announced that he was returning to Oklahoma City to form a law practice with Whit Pate, a former legal assistant to Governor J. Howard Edmondson. During these years of law practice, Murray worked as an attorney for the state welfare department, the agency he was so critical of in the *Saturday Evening Post* article.[49]

Although he remained close to politics, Murray never served in political office after he left the governor's office. He remained a Democrat, but like his father, he would not always remain faithful to the party. In 1956, while still in Texas, Murray joined a movement of Democrats for President Dwight D. Eisenhower, then seeking reelection. It was not that he refused to support Adlai E. Stevenson, again the Democratic candidate, whom he had actively campaigned for in 1952. Murray seemed to have been caught up in the Eisenhower campaign, which had so much support among Texas Democrats. It also gave him a chance to campaign, and he made several appearances, using his skill in the Spanish language to speak to Mexican-American audiences in Texas. Murray tried to make a political comeback after he returned to Oklahoma. In 1962, he ran for the Democratic nomination for state treasurer, but he failed to earn even a spot for the runoff primary. Murray died on April 16, 1974, and was buried in Tishomingo.[50]

If change is to be the gauge by which the Murray administration is measured, it cannot be considered a success, for no major changes occurred during his term in office. Murray himself set the tone of his administration by campaigning on a platform which could be considered a status quo approach to government. His stands on economy in government and no new taxes struck a responsive chord of conservatism in Oklahoma voters, who seemed willing to accept the current situation.

Despite his conservative platform, however, Murray must be considered a reformer. While in office, he spoke of good government and reform as if he were still campaigning for the vote. Somehow, it seemed that he believed he would win success for his reform measures by gaining public support for them. Yet it would not be the voters with whom he had to deal to ensure the success of his proposals.

Persuasive speeches were evidently not enough to win the necessary legislative support for the type of governmental reform Murray advocated. Such an undertaking required a strong bond between Murray and the legislature, but this he was unable to provide. Perhaps at least part of Murray's ineptness at working with the legislature was due to the fact that he had not come up through legislative ranks to become governor, but inexperience cannot be blamed entirely for Murray's poor relationship with the legislature.

To call Murray a weak governor does not offer an adequate explanation of why so little of his program won acceptance. His forceful and frequent use of the veto indicates strength, so perhaps he was out of step with his own political times. By the way he presented his proposals, which he strongly supported, it would seem that he would have been more comfortable as governor in a time when the executive and legislative branches of government were separated in practice as well as in theory. He indicated he was unwilling or unable to become involved in the transactions that had earlier been reserved exclusively for legislators. Perhaps it was because this side of government did not interest him.

Whatever the reasons, as it became evident that Murray's plans to reform Oklahoma's government were destined for failure, he resorted only to stronger language. This response merely weakened his position with the legislature, thus ensuring his program to doom, despite the urgent need the state had for many of his proposals.

ENDNOTES

[1] Johnston Murray and Al Dewlen, "Oklahoma is in a Mess!", *Saturday Evening Post*, Vol. CCXXVII, No. 44 (April 30, 1955), p. 20.

[2] *Ibid.*

[3] *Daily Oklahoman* (Oklahoma City), January 9, 1950, p. 1, 2; Keith L. Bryant, Jr., *Alfalfa Bill Murray* (Norman: University of Oklahoma Press, 1968), pp. 150,154.

[4] *Daily Oklahoman*, January 9, 1950, pp. 1, 2; *Tulsa Tribune* (Tulsa), January 9, 1950, pp. 1, 2; William H. Murray to Johnston Murray, January 9, 1950, Johnston Murray Collection, Western History Collections, University of Oklahoma, Norman, Oklahoma; *Daily Oklahoman*, May 7, 1950, pp. 1, 23.

[5] *Daily Oklahoman*, May 19, 1950, p. 11, May 24, 1950, p. 18, July 5, 1950, p. 1.

[6] Martin Hauan Interview, June 19, 1976, Oklahoma City, Oklahoma. Hauan served as Murray's press secretary.

[7] *Daily Oklahoman*, July 6, 1950, p. 2; *Tulsa Tribune*, July 6, 1950, p. 23.

[8] *Tulsa Tribune*, July 17, 1950, p. 7; *Daily Oklahoman*, July 11, 1950, p. 1, July 17, 1950, p. 1, July 18, 1950, p. 7, July 19, 1950, p. 1.

[9] *Daily Oklahoman*, July 30, 1950, p. 1, August 10, 1950, p. 1; *Tulsa Tribune*, July 31, 1950, p. 1.

[10] Oklahoma House, *Journal of the House of Representatives, Twenty-third Legislature, Regular Session, 1951* (Oklahoma City: Leader Press, 1951), p. 9.

[11] *Daily Oklahoman*, January 13, 1951, p. 7.

[12] *Ibid.*, April 10, 1951, p. 1, May 10, 1951, p. 1, December 16, 1952, pp. 1, 8, June 25, 1953, p. 4, June 30, 1953, p. 1.

[13] Lee Slater, comp., *Directory of Oklahoma, 1975* (Oklahoma City: Oklahoma State Election Board, 1975), pp. 533, 534.

[14] *Daily Oklahoman*, March 21, 1951, p. 1; Joe Hubbell, "A History of the Oklahoma Education Association, 1945-1965," (Doctor of Education Dissertation, Stillwater: Oklahoma State University, 1970), pp. 270, 280; *Daily Oklahoman*, April 19, 1951, p. 1.

[15] *Daily Oklahoman*, March 28, 1951, p. 3, January 6, 1952, p. 4-B; Hubbell, "A History of the Oklahoma Education Association, 1945-1965," p. 274.

[16] *Daily Oklahoman*, April 8, 1951, pp. 1, 2.

[17] *Ibid..*

[18] *Ibid.*, August 16, 1951, p. 8, January 9, 1955, p. 2.

[19] *Ibid.*, January 6, 1952, p. 4-B, July 30, 1952, p. 13, July 31, 1952, p. 12.

[20] *Ibid.*, November 9, 1951, p. 1.

[23] Oklahoma House, *Journal of the House of Representatives, Twenty-fourth Legislature, Regular Session, 1953* (Oklahoma City: Leader Press, 1953), pp. 36, 37, 38, 43.

[24] *Ibid.*, pp. 43, 44, 45.

[25] *Ibid.*, p. 54.

[26] *Ibid.*, pp. 146-147.

[27] *Daily Oklahoman*, March 1, 1953, pp. 1-B, 2-B.

[28] *Ibid.*, April 16, 1953, p. 1, July 21, 1953, p. 1.

[29] Oklahoma House, *Journal of the House of Representatives, 1953*, pp. 1288-1289.

[30] *Daily Oklahoman*, January 9, 1955, pp. 1, 2; Hubbell, "A History of the Oklahoma Education Association, 1945-1965," pp. 278-280.

[31] Victor E. Harlow, *Oklahoma History* (Oklahoma City: Harlow Publishing Corporation, 1961), p. 502; *Daily Oklahoman*, April 24, 1953, p. 1, May 8, 1953, p. 12.

[32] Oklahoma House, *Journal of the House of Representatives, 1953*, p. 1739.

[33] *Ibid.*, p. 1738.

[34] *Daily Oklahoman*, October 26, 1953, p. 1.

[35] *Ibid.*, January 27, 1954, p. 1; Martin Hauan Interview, June 29, 1976.

36 Martin Hauan Interview, June 29, 1976; *Daily Oklahoman*, May 28, 1954, p. 6.

37 *Daily Oklahoman*, June 11, 1954, p. 34.

38 Martin Hauan Interview, June 29, 1976.

39 *Daily Oklahoman*, January 30, 1954, p. 1.

40 *Ibid.*, July 3, 1954, p. 1, July 7, 1954, p. 17, July 13, 1954, p. 1.

41 *Ibid.*, July 13, 1954, p. 1, January 9, 1955, p. 1, August 26, 1954, p. 12.

42 Oklahoma House, *Journal of the House of Representatives, Twenty-fifth Legislature, Regular Session* (Oklahoma City: Leader Press, 1955), pp. 44-59.

43 Al Dewlen to Johnston Murray, January 3, 1955, Johnston Murray Collection, Western History Collections, University of Oklahoma, Norman.

44 Murray and Dewlen, "Oklahoma is in a Mess!", *Saturday Evening Post*, Vol. CCXXVII, No. 44, p. 21.

45 *Ibid.*, pp. 92, 96, 20.

46 Martin Hauan Interview, June 29, 1976.

47 Murray and Dewlen, "Oklahoma is in a Mess!", *Saturday Evening Post*, Vol. CCXXVII, No. 44, p. 96.

48 *Daily Oklahoman*, September 27, 1955, p. 1, October 7, 1955, p. 1; Martin Hauan Interview, June 29, 1976; *Daily Oklahoman*, February 29, 1956, p. 1, April 17, 1974, p. 19.

49 *Daily Oklahoman*, August 18, 1954, p. 9, January 19, 1958, p. 1, February 9, 1960, p. 1.

50 Martin Hauan Interview, June 29, 1976; *Daily Oklahoman*, April 17, 1974, p. 19.

Oklahoma Highway Department: during Holloway administration, 5, 38-
39, 44, 46-47; during Kerr administration, 20, 133; during Turner
administration, 24, 167; during Johnston Murray administration, 192
Oklahoma Highway Patrol: established
during Marland administration, 11,
97
Oklahoma Historical Society: new building dedicated by Holloway, 47-48;
assisted by Turner, 170
Oklahoma House of Representatives:
56, 84, 104, 105, 106; during Holloway administration, 4, 39-43; during
Marland administration, 10, 89, 90,
91, 92-93, 95; during Phillips administration, 14, 30, 108, 109, 110, 111,
116; during Johnston Murray administration, 27, 28, 179, 181, 184, 185-
186, 187, 190; during Johnston administration, 31; during William H.
Murray administration, 60; during
Kerr administration, 129, 131, 135,
136; during Turner administration,
160, 164-166; see also Oklahoma Legislature and Oklahoma Senate
Oklahoma Human Services Department:
see Oklahoma Public Welfare Department
"Oklahoma is in a Mess!": Johnston
Murray's article published in Saturday
Evening Post, 28-29, 174, 191-193
Oklahoma Land Commission: served by
Johnston Murray as secretary, 26,
168, 176
Oklahoma Legislature: 56, 152; during
Holloway administration, 3, 4, 5, 36,
39-43; during Marland administration, 10, 11, 12, 85-93, 94, 95-97, 98;
during Phillips administration, 14,
16-17, 18, 105, 106, 108-109, 110,
111, 114-116; during Kerr administration, 18-20, 21, 129-133, 135, 136,
140, 145, 146; during Turner administration, 22-25, 155-156, 157, 158-
160, 162-167, 168, 170; during Johnston Murray administration, 26-29,
174, 179-181, 183-187, 189, 190, 191,
192, 193, 195; during Johnston administration, 35; during William H.
Murray administration, 60, 61, 66-67,
69; see also Oklahoma House of Representatives and Oklahoma Senate
Oklahoma Mental Health Board: see
Oklahoma Board of Mental Health
Oklahoma National Guard: during Wil-

liam H. Murray administration, 6-7,
29, 62, 63-64; during Phillips administration, 15, 29, 112-113; during Holloway administration, 31-32; during
Johnston administration, 35; during
Marland administration, 90; supported
by Kerr, 126; Johnston Murray resigns
commission, 177; during Johnston
Murray administration, 190-191
Oklahoma Pardon and Parole Board:
established during Kerr administration, 18, 21, 130, 131, 146; beginning
made during Holloway administration,
44
Oklahoma Penitentiary: during Phillips
administration, 119; during Turner
administration, 160
Oklahoma Planning and Resources
Board: established during Marland
administration, 11, 91; during Turner
administration, 22, 158
Oklahoma Press Association: addressed
by Johnston Murray, 189
Oklahoma Public Affairs Board: see
Oklahoma Board of Public Affairs
Oklahoma Public Safety Department:
established during Marland administration, 11, 97
Oklahoma Public Welfare Commission:
during Phillips administration, 110-
111
Oklahoma Public Welfare Department
(Oklahoma Human Services Depart-
ment): during Turner administration,
162; during Johnston Murray administration, 192; employs Johnston
Murray, 194
Oklahoma Retailers Association: addressed by Johnston Murray, 187
Oklahoma School Bond Retirement
Fund: created during Kerr administration, 130
Oklahoma School Land Department:
during Kerr administration, 130
Oklahoma School Land Office: during
Holloway administration, 5, 44
Oklahoma Senate: 33-34; during Marland administration, 10, 89-90, 95;
during Johnston Murray administration, 27, 179, 180, 181; during Johnston administration, 31, 35; during
Holloway administration, 39-43; during William H. Murray administration, 67; during Phillips administration, 108, 109-110, 111, 116; during
Kerr administration, 129, 131, 135;
during Turner administration, 160,

The text of *Oklahoma's Governors, 1929-1955: Depression to Prosperity*, has been set in eleven-point Andover. Two points of line spacing have been added for increased legibility. The text and illustrations have been printed by offset on paper which has an intended effective life of at least three hundred years. Printed in the United States of America.